The Myth of Democracy

The Myth of
DEMOCRACY

by Ferdinand Lundberg

A Lyle Stuart Book
Published by Carol Publishing Group

TO ELIZABETH

Copyright © 1989 Ferdinand Lundberg

A Lyle Stuart Book
Published by Carol Publishing Group

Editorial Offices
600 Madison Avenue
New York, NY 10022

Sales & Distribution Offices
120 Enterprise Avenue
Secaucus, NJ 07094

In Canada: Musson Book Company
A division of General Publishing Co. Limited
Don Mills, Ontario

Manufactured in the United States of America

Library of Congress Cataloging-in-Publication Data

Lundberg, Ferdinand, 1902–
     The myth of democracy / by Ferdinand Lundberg.
       p.   cm.
     ISBN 0-8184-0500-7 : $11.95
       1. Representative government and representation—United States.
     2. United States—Politics and government. 3. Democracy.
     I. Title.
JK1071.L86 1989
320.973—dc20
                                                              89-11291
                                                                  CIP

I

DEMOCRACY is the flaming watchword of the age, beloved of hard-eyed politicians and starry-eyed professors, soothing to the masses and happily claimed as a self-description by virtually all governments, especially ironclad dictatorships. The word in practice has truly become a synonym for any kind of government.

Yet it nowhere exists—or ever existed—in the sense that a given government is either "by the people" or clearly "for the people" although it is always "of the people." A constant chorus of complaints against governors all over the world shows this. If the people were really governing, against whom are the complainers complaining? It is evident from many of the complaints that the people feel powerless, quite out of control.

In fact, democracy nowhere exists in any of the senses implied by its most vocal devotees. Against the background of reality it is a fantasy. It is one of a number of secular myths that flourish simultaneously. Mythic thinking is by no means obsolete in this scientific age. More people than not are addicted to one grandiose myth or the other, as the celebrants of democrary show. Science and the scientific outlook, or just plain common sense, are the instrumentalities of a relatively small number of people who are rarely encountered face to face.

Because just about every contemporary government, including left wing and right wing dictatorships, claims to be a democracy, it seems desirable to determine precisely what democracy is supposed to be. The term "left wing dictatorship" is an internally contradictory journalistic construction. Leftism always connoted greater freedom from authority and rightism stressed authority. But all dictatorships are essentially the same, whether designated as right or left, as belonging to workers or to proprietors. Essentially, too, they all restrict workers.

What was first to be designated as democracy appeared in ancient Athens in the 5th century B.C. The word derived from the Greek *demos*, meaning people, and *kratein*, meaning to rule, related to *kratos*, meaning authority. The word came into use as part of a political restructuring to bring more people into government in order to defend against threatened Persian invasions.

Athens also built a very effective navy, which enabled it to assume a protective role for some 200 Greek city-states. In this connection it organized the Delian League of city-states, membership in which was initially voluntary. But in the course of time, membership became compulsory as Athens placed garrisons throughout what became known as the Athenian Empire.

Athens insisted upon installing its democratic structure in all the Delian city-states, although policy for the whole was made only in Athens. All these city-states, including Athens, previously had been under the rule of one man, called a tyrant, plus a group of close followers. Although now a word with sinister implications, the word tyrant, originally *tyrannos*, meant no more than lord or chief and most tyrants ruled more or less with popular consent.

In the Athenian city-state, the popularly elected assembly made all the laws. Political offices were filled by lot. Under Pericles from 461 to 429 B.C., an innovation was the payment of all public servants out of imperial funds to which all League members contributed, thus attracting people to seek public office as a source of income. However, the number of eligible voters in Athens never exceeded 43,000 men. Excluded from voting were about the same number of women, some 28,000 resident aliens and some 110,000 slaves—largely military captives or their descendants. But also excluded from voting in the central Athens forum was any representation of the Delian empire outside Athens.

In actual fact, far from having the government driven by the voting populace, as is commonly supposed, the leaders with the support of a majority of the assembly votes ruled the Athenian empire, as in Britain today. And according to the Greek historian Thucydides, who lived in the same period under the leadership of Pericles, what was nominally a democracy became in fact one-man rule or at least representational republican government. So that, at the very inception, the story begins to assume an all-too-familiar clouded complexion.

At the end of the 5th century, Sparta and its landbased allies felt threatened by Athenian prosperity and expansion. They destroyed the Athenian empire, thus ending all pretense of democracy for more than two millennia.

The idea of democracy, seemingly dead beyond recall, surfaced again in revolutionary 17th century Britain, a time of civil war and tremendous political turmoil. Just about every conceivable political idea received some sort of written sponsorship in a great variety of journals and pamphlets, among them a vastly romanticized version of long-dead Athenian democracy. But it was in Britain that the concept of popular sovereignty exploded into modern view. Later, it surfaced in France and in the newborn United States.

Democracy became one of a long procession of political panaceas, eventually coming full circle in the idea of government-centered socialism.

But in colonial New England, settled by Puritans from the 17th century Puritan revolution in England, modern democracy had its first genuine test in the town meetings. These town meetings consisted of the entire male citizenry and were simply the legislature for the town, with a majority vote prevailing in the establishment of laws and appointment of town officers. Here, more than anywhere else, one found genuine democracy at work although it was not the system for the colonial province itself, with its Crown-appointed governor and judges.

Government in New England was entirely the affair of men. Although a few women like Abigail Adams, wife of John Adams, objected to the exclusion of women from politics, her view doesn't appear to have been shared by many other women. Blacks and Indians, too, were not included among "the people."

At any rate, in colonial New England, the towns were governed by an unalloyed direct democratic system, perhaps the first and only time ever in the history of the world.

II

BY THE TIME of the American Constitutional Convention of 1787, it was established that democracy consisted of popular voting pure and simple, either for officers of various kinds including legislators or for laws and public policies. A majority of voters, democrats felt, could do no wrong (as people are predominantly "good") and in many of the states that were former English colonies this attitude prevailed.

In such states, sympathizers with the lawfully established English governments were, on the basis of popular votes, deprived of their property by simple confiscation. This revolutionary happening had a profound effect on the writers of the United States Constitution, who incorporated in it provisions that made such a procedure virtually impossible again. And such restrictive provisions, as James Madison expressed it, were designed to prevent a "tyranny of the majority," an emerging new concept. After the secession from Great Britain, the former owners of confiscated property were reimbursed by the newly-founded United States

Madison, often erroneously styled the "father" of the Constitution, no doubt had the New England colonies and early Greek city-states in mind when he wrote in No. 10 of *The Federalist Papers* that a pure democracy is "a society consisting of a small number of citizens, who assemble and administer the government in person ..."

The Constitution of the United States did not provide for this sort of government but for a republic which, Madison wrote, is a "government in which the scheme of representation takes place." In other words, if there is representation of the voters that is no democracy because the representative can, and often does, act according to his own notions.

In the same publication, Madison also said that "The two great points of difference between a democracy and a republic are the delegation of the government in the latter, to a small number of citizens elected by the rest; secondly, the greater number of citizens and greater sphere of country over which the latter may be extended."

So, contrary to what is widely taught in the schools of the United States and bruited about in the news media and expressions of politicians, the United States is *not*—in the opinion of one of its principal founders and interpreters—a democracy. The Constitution itself, Article IV, Section 4, says: "The United States shall guarantee to every State in this Union a Republican form of government..." Taken simply literally it is a guarantee of a republican government *in* the states and a republican government *outside* and *above* the states. There is no mention of the word democracy in the Constitution.

But, devotees of the word "democracy" may object, the Constitution today is very changed from its original form. Under it, it may be argued, democracy has flowered, presenting us with the vote-producing political machines of New York City, Chicago, Boston, Philadelphia and an assortment of other localities. In all those places one may find grass roots democracy at work, it is contended.

Democracy was not highly rated by the writers of the Constitution. This fact emerged early in the proceedings of the Constitutional Convention when the method of choosing the members of the House of Representatives was discussed on May 31, 1787. The notes of Delegate James McHenry of Maryland, dated May 29, stated, "Our chief danger arises from the democratic parts of our [state] constitutions. It is a maxim which I hold incontrovertible, that the powers of government exercised by the people swallow up the other branches. None of the constitutions have provided sufficient checks against the democracy."

According to Madison's notes about House elections, Roger Sherman of Connecticut, who had started his career as a shoemaker, "opposed the election by the people, insisting that it ought to be by the [State] Legislatures." The people, he said, "[immediately] should have as little to do as may be about the Government. They want information and are constantly liable to be misled."

Madison now quotes Elbridge Gerry of Massachusetts, who said: "The evils we experience flow from the excess of democracy. The people do not want virtue; but are the dupes of pretended patriots. In Massts. it has been fully confirmed by experience that they are daily misled into the most baneful measures and opinions by the false reports circulated by designing men, and which no one on the spot can refute. One principal evil arises from the want of due provision for those employed in the administration of Government.

"It would seem to be a maxim of democracy to starve the public servants. He mentioned the popular clamour in Massachusetts for the reduction of salaries and the attack made on that of the Govr. though secured by the spirit of the Constitution itself. He had he said been too republican heretofore: he was still however republican, but he had been taught by experience the danger of the levilling spirit."

Convention members now split, some favoring popular election of House members and others not. George Mason of Virginia, James Wilson of Pennsylvania, leading theoretician of the Convention, and Madison himself favored popular election of the House but many members registered strong dissent. On the vote, six states favored House elections by the people, two voted against and two were divided in their votes. In short, democratic elections for one house of Congress were not generally approved.

Governor Edmund Randolph of Virginia, who proposed what was known as the Virginia Plan for a constitution, "observed that the general object was to provide a cure for the evils under which the U.S. laboured; that in tracing these evils to their origin every man had found it in the turbulence and follies of democracy: that some check therefore was to be sought for agst. this tendency of our Governments: and that a good Senate seemed most likely to answer the purpose."

These citations all come from *The Records of the Federal Convention of 1787*, edited by Max Farrand.*

The problems of the Convention, as its leaders saw them, were not to establish or to safeguard democracy in the Constitution but to bridle and subdue it. And this was done in the Constitution of the United States with a view to making it a more balanced instrument, so that tyranny could not be promoted in the name of democracy.

---

*1937 revised edition, Vol. I, Yale University Press.

III

ALTHOUGH the Constitution-makers of 1787 thought they had hogtied democracy, they reckoned without Thomas Jefferson. This author of the *Declaration of Independence* had been Minister to France during the writing of the U.S. Constitution but he was appointed the first Secretary of State by President George Washington, the only unopposed presidential candidate in United States history.

In this office, Jefferson clashed almost at once with Alexander Hamilton. Jefferson had reservations about the Constitution, feeling it did not sufficiently safeguard the rights of individuals. But this doubt was put to rest with the quick adoption of the first ten Amendments. He disagreed with Hamilton, the Secretary of the Treasury, over the establishment of the Bank of the United States, which Jefferson feared would favor the financial interests and would corrupt the legislature. After hearing both men, Washington sided with Hamilton the pragmatist against Jefferson the ideologist.

The two men had totally different visions of the future. Hamilton saw the country as a great manufacturing and commercial center and Jefferson saw it as mainly agrarian and composed of small independent farmers, the core of the Jeffersonian democracy. Jefferson, because of his European experience, was hostile to large cities and their industrial-commercial operatives. He was also distrustful of concentrated power. At the end of 1793, frustrated at every turn by Hamilton, Jefferson resigned.

Opponents of Hamilton, mainly agrarian, had collected in sufficient numbers to proclaim themselves Republicans and to see Jefferson as their leader. Jefferson and many of his followers were sympathetic to the French Revolution. In this, the United States was officially neutral. Hamilton, for his part, favored England, mainly for national financial reasons.

Jefferson was supported by the Republicans for President in 1796. Running second to John Adams by three electoral votes, he became Vice President. Republican forces now solidified behind him and approved his opposition to the repressive Alien and Sedition Laws of the Adams Administration. He and Madison also stood forth as partisans of "states rights" against the federal system in the Kentucky and Virginia Resolutions, the former written by Jefferson and the latter by Madison.

Jefferson was elected President in 1800 under the banner of what was now called the Democratic-Republican Party. As President, he came out strongly against the way judicial power of the United States was used. In general his policies stimulated rank-and-file political activism so that it was largely under Jefferson that the Democratic Party took form as distinguished from the earlier Federalists. However, the government was held within constitutional bounds mainly by the Supreme Court which under Chief Justice John Marshall had found a role for itself in interpreting the Constitution.

From Jefferson onward, every successful candidate for President ran under the Democratic-Republican designation up to John Quincy Adams in 1824, and after that under simply the designation of Democratic until Martin Van Buren in 1836. But thereafter, until the election of Abraham Lincoln as a Republican in 1860, the Democrats won all elections except those of 1840 and 1848, which were won by Whigs, a group precursor to the Lincoln Republicans.

And thereafter until 1912, excepting the elections of 1884 and 1892, the Republican Party steadily won national elections.

The criterion for determining whether democracy is present or not in the American system is the voting franchise and this was not significantly altered until the 19th Amendment to the Constitution in 1920 gave the national vote to women. The voting age for males and females was lowered from 21 to 18 by the 26th Amendment in 1971. For a brief period after the Civil War, Negroes were allowed to vote under 13th, 14th and 15th Amendments to the Constitution but an inter-party deal in 1876 enabled the southern states thereafter to inhibit the voting of Negroes by a variety of technical devices such as illiteracy. At the same time, illiterate whites were welcomed as voters. In effect, black voting was stopped throughout the South.

Despite the broadening of the franchise, which democrats regard as essential to solving all ills, seldom does slightly more than half the eligible electorate vote in national elections. Far less than half vote in intermediate and local elections. The franchise, in fact, was broadened not in response to any popular demand but at the demand of scattered ideologists.

Many non-voters are from among the uneducated but many highly sophisticated persons in the United States do not vote because they see little difference between the two parties, which have become increasingly Centrist because a position at or near the center insures the most votes. Bright ideas that are away from the center in either direction do not attract as many votes as they lose, so they are usually shunned by both parties.

However, the stimulation of popular voting frenzy by the Jeffersonians long before women or teenagers were allowed to vote and with no assistance from blacks, did have profound structural effects on the governments of the states. These had been uniformly patterned on the governments of the United States, as though turned out with a cookie cutter—except for Nebraska which has a unicameral legislature. All the other states are bicameral, with a governor and a court system extending from high to low. Although the various state constitutions have different peripheral provisions, they are all basically copies of the system provided in the United States constitution.

But there are fundamental differences. The sharpest between the Federal and the state governments is found in the judiciary. None of the original states allowed popular election of judges. In seven states, judicial selection was exercised by the legislatures and six entrusted such selection to a combination of the governor and either the legislature or an executive council.

"With the eruption of Jacksonian Democracy in the 1820s and 1830s, one state after another switched to an elective system. Judges were elected in Georgia as early as 1812. Mississippi, in 1832, became the first state with an all-elective judiciary. From 1846, when New York decided to elect its judges, until Alaska joined the Union in 1958, every new state arrived with a provision for an elected judiciary."[1]

But owing to repeated charges by office-seekers, scandals and outright cases of corruption of judges, a number of states reinstated the appointive system and others sought a solution in what is known as the non-partisan ballot or some variation thereof. Judicial elections produced in the states what was very much like an open running sewer, a constant source of resounding scandals. Democracy here became a self-defeating and destructive travesty.

As matters now stand, all states except ten have some form of public election of judges. The ten where the governor, the legislature or some combination of both appoint judges are mainly on the Atlantic seaboard: Delaware, Connecticut, Maine, Massachusetts, New Hampshire, New Jersey, Rhode Island, South Carolina, Virginia and Hawaii. Except for Hawaii, these were all territorially part of the original 13 states and were represented by stripes on the American flag.

Sixteen states still elect judges by partisan ballot and in some of these judicial scandals are still a matter of common occurrence. These states are given by Donald Dale Jackson as Alabama, Georgia, Louisiana, Arkansas, New Mexico, New York, North Carolina, Tennessee, Texas, Mississippi, Maryland, West Virginia, Kansas, Indiana and Pennsylvania. To these 15, Illinois should be added.

Fifteen states have what is called a non-partisan ballot—that is, elections without party designation although usually nominations are made by the established parties. And political parties and a variety of pressure groups may make themselves felt informally as in openly partisan elections. Using this system are: Arizona, California, Idaho, Kentucky, Michigan, Minnesota, Montana, Nevada, North Dakota, Ohio, Oregon, Oklahoma, South Dakota, Washington and Wisconsin.

---

[1] Donald Dale Jackson, *Judges: An Inside View of the Agonies and Excesses of an American Elite*, New York, Atheneum, 1974, p.15.

Then, nine states use a reform-scheme known since 1940 as the "Missouri Plan" in which a judicial selection commission presents a list of eligibles to the governor, who then appoints, with a public election held at a later date. In this way, it is hoped, freelance predators or political cat's paws are kept out of the judiciary. The states that employ this method or some variant thereof are Colorado, Iowa, Missouri, Nebraska, Utah, Alaska, Wyoming, Vermont and Florida.

Yet none of the states using the method of public election has achieved the judicial tranquillity of either the Federal system or of the states using the appointive system exclusively.

Observers often express wonder that the Federal judiciary has existed for 200 years on all its levels with surprisingly few delinquents. There should be no mystery about why this is so. First, Federal judicial appointments are for life. By contrast, nearly all state judges serve for stipulated terms, subject to re-election.

The Federal appointment is obviously the one to be more highly prized. In Massachusetts and New Hampshire, appointed judges serve until age 70—in effect for life. Federal judges are usually better paid than state judges and enjoy more prestige. Elected state judges enjoy no greater public standing than do governors, mayors or legislators, about whom a large public has become cynical. Finally, Federal appointments are usually made of more established or reputable figures.

This is not to say that the Federal bench is untrammeled by politics. "Political scientist John Schmidhauser found that 49 of the first 91 Supreme Court justices were 'lawyers who were primarily politicians.' Twenty-four were primarily judges, all were corporation lawyers, and three were non-corporate attorneys. Only four—Roosevelt's four—were professional teachers."[2]

But few Federal judges have carried their political partisanship onto the bench. What there is of bias in Federal judges appears to consist mainly of their liberal or conservative orientations, and these terms themselves are not very precise.

Most knowledgeable American lawyers appear to admire English judges more than American. And English judges are

---

[2] *Ibid.*, 15-16.

appointed. But those seeking a better way might turn to the French system, which obtains judges the way we obtain scientists and military officers—by educating them as such. Like American generals and admirals, French judges attend special schools. Upon graduation they are given assignments in the lower reaches of the judicial system and over the years work their way upward. They are neither appointed nor elected but are *assigned* and serve until retirement. If the United States really wanted better judges, it could adopt the French system. It is doubtful, however, if the democratic mass has any particuar feeling about judges one way or the other.

Just how unbelievably bad a state judicial system may become will be seen by taking note of a few cases.

As of August 8, 1988, the 14th Chicago and Cook County judge was brought to trial in the aftermath of a Federal investigation extending back several years. In these trials, 12 judges and 55 lawyers and court officials were convicted and imprisoned for corruption—consisting of giving and taking money for rendering favorable court decisions contrary to law and evidence. One other judge committed suicide.

The method of operation was for lawyers to split their fees with judges, who presumably shared with party organizations. The lawyers, owing to their success with difficult cases, were able to charge big fees for little real work. Clients, who did not necessarily know the decisions were bought, may in some cases have thought the lawyers had unusual expertise.

While this Federal investigation was welcome to many local observers, it was true that journalists in the Chicago area had been suspicious about the Cook County judiciary for 60 years. What was found in Operation Graylord, the code name of the investigation, was simply the latest phase of a corrupt political system that was firmly in place.

In Illinois, judges are elected by districts, not voted upon "at large" or state wide. Nine states elect judges by districts and where this is done it is much easier to concentrate political influence. It is more difficult to use influence where elections are "at large" because a broader background must be reckoned with. As Cook County, like the five New York City counties, always contains a heavily foreign and external transferee population, it is easily manipulated by politicians. This is also true of other large cities.

There is much more to know about irregularity in the Illinois judicial system but similar conditions are found in other states. In New York State, for example, irregularities are regularly brought to light. In 1986, Federal Judge Jack B. Weinstein sentenced former New York State Supreme Court Justice William C. Brennan to five years in prison, five years probation and fined him $209,000 for taking bribes to "fix" criminal cases. The New York Supreme Court corresponds to what is called the Superior Court in many states. *The New York Times*, which is usually quite reserved editorially, the next day denounced the sentence as too lenient in view of the magnitude of Judge Brennan's offenses.

As in the case of Illinois, to give any adequate account of judicial irregularities in New York State or Texas would require a book in itself.

In Brooklyn in 1987, suspended Civil Court Judge Samuel Weinberg pleaded guilty to racketeering charges and agreed to forfeit $500,000 in illegal proceeds. He was charged with arson, extortion and other crimes prior to assuming his position on the bench. He was, in fact, a pre-bench criminal.

Anyone who doubts that the situation is bad or who believes that I exaggerate should read *Judges* by Donald Dale Jackson, *The Finest Judges Money Can Buy* by Chuck Ashman, or *The Corrupt Judge* by Joseph Borkin.

As to the general character of state judges: it is about equal to that of other elected officials, and in a scattered range from zero to 100. In the case of Federal judges, the prevalent public opinion is that they are, in general, more trustworthy and professionally informed than the general run of Federal officeholder. These latter, up to the level of President, can be quite deficient, as evidenced by such examples as Warren Harding and Gerald Ford. The record, at any rate, shows a vast difference between elected state judges and Federal judges.

However, it is not the corruption or misconduct of some elected judges that mainly calls into question the wisdom of electing judges. The mere fact that a judge must keep in mind voter approval in order to retain his seat trammels many of his decisions. The reason this is so is that it is agreed by all experts that a judge should render disinterested decisions based on law and valid evidence. For his own continuance in office to depend on the nature of some of his decisions, whether or not they please the electorate, automatically contaminates certain decisions.

An election, the hallmark of democracy, is seen then as an undesirable enterprise when it comes to electing a judge or set of judges.

IV

JUDGES OF ANY KIND are all drawn from the large pool of American lawyers. And so we come to another revealing facet of American democracy. It is commonly thought that lawyers belong to a learned profession. And, true enough, a number of lawyers are indeed learned. But if they are it is purely a matter of their own inclination and volition. For there is no formal legal or institutional pressure upon them, at least in the United States, to be learned. Medical doctors or university professors are usually highly learned, and the medical doctors are required to be so in every state in order to get a license to practice.

Since Colonial days, the feeling has grown that the legal profession should be readily accessible to every man. This is considered the democratic way: any man or woman a lawyer. And in various states all anyone may still do is "read" law in the office of a lawyer and after a time apply for admission to the bar. With the application one submits the names of members of the bar who vouch for the applicant's "good character." In practice, good character means one has never been accused of a crime.

Some states require applicants to pass relatively stiff bar examinations, and New York is one of these. But many states stage easy examinations. It is, furthermore, not generally the case that the states require lawyers to have a university background. Both in New York and Illinois, and in other states as well, there are what are called night law schools. These are mainly patronized by employed persons, more particularly by clerical employees of municipal, county, state and Federal government departments. Such schools uphold the ideal of democracy: any man a lawyer. And such schools produce acceptably proficient lawyers. But the lawyers they produce have, in general, what one would call a "thin" degree.

Much "heavier" degrees are issued by the leading university law schools, which also require a general college degree. Yet while learning may rightly be regarded as a partial guarantee of probity—at least that the degree holder will take the long view at all times—it is by no means an infallible sign of rectitude or competence.

Francis Bacon, one of England's leading philosophers, as Lord Chancellor (chief judge) of England was convicted of corruption in 1621, was fined £40,000, imprisoned in the Tower of London and barred from office for life. The charges were brought by political enemies, themselves no angels. Part of the defense was that it was customary to receive gifts on the bench, which was true. Even though Bacon's accusers were themselves less than pure the verdict nevertheless stood and Bacon made a full confession. His imprisonment and fine were remitted. His enemies were satisfied just to get him out of the way.

Nearer to us in time and place is the story of highly educated Otto Kerner, of the Seventh Circuit United States Court of Appeals—a lofty post but less lofty than Bacon's. The son of a Federal judge, Kerner was brought up in affluent circumstances and had a distinguished career. He was an alumnus of Brown University, Cambridge University (England) and Northwestern University Law School. He was first a United States Attorney, then a Cook County judge and then a two-term Illinois governor before his elevation to the United States Court of Appeals. He attained national prominence in 1967 by heading what became known as the Kerner Commission to study and report on race relations.

Yet in 1974, Judge Kerner entered prison after having been convicted on 17 counts of bribery, perjury, tax evasion and mail fraud. His sentence was for three years plus a fine of $50,000. His defense was that he, a Federal judge, had been duped by shrewd operators.

So formal education alone is no guarantee of rectitude. It should make a person more reflective than the rabble, and thoughtful with respect to his family. It is the families of elevated miscreants who suffer most as they almost always have an exaggerated esteem for the fallen. The family members are usually highly sheltered and law-abiding. Then, suddenly, they are forced to choose either the side of the revealed culprit or society. The resulting emotional strain is often intense.

Author Joseph Borkin found only 55 cases in which Federal judges were investigated for some sort of misconduct. Forty-four were settled without trial or impeachment; eight were censured, 17 resigned and others were either absolved or their cases died in committee. Eight went to trial on impeachment; four were convicted. Only one, Federal Appellate Judge Martin Manton—another highly educated character—went to prison.

Since Borkin's book, three Federal judges have been dethroned for corruption—Harry C. Claiborne, jailed and removed by Senate vote; Walter L. Nixon, convicted of perjury and bribery; and the nonpareil Otto Kerner.

The pool of lawyers from which judges are drawn in the United States is very large. In 1986, there were 655,191 lawyers in the country, according to the *U.S. Statistical Abstract, 1988*. Of these, 53,035 were employed in government, with 33,046 at the state, county and local levels. Additionally, there were 21,677 in judicial assignments—3,003 at the Federal level and the remainder state, county and city. A total of 460,206 lawyers were in private practice and 83,843 were salaried in private industry, educational institutions or other private bodies. Finally, 36,430 were classified as inactive or retired.

There is the greatest concentration of lawyers in the District of Columbia—28,399 or one lawyer for every 22 members of the population. New York has the most lawyers at 72,575 or one lawyer for 244 of state poplulation, the narrowest lawyer-to-population ratio of any state by a wide margin. California, Illinois and Texas are next in line respectively.

The American political system, in brief, has lawyers posted at every turn and could not function for a day without lawyers. Lawyers are among the advisers of every political figure and these figures are themselves often lawyers. Most of the writers of the Constitution originally were lawyers—33 of 55 who checked in, although only 39 delegates remained to sign—and every step in the amending process has been supervised by lawyers. At all times, most members of Congress are lawyers and most members of state legislatures and local legislative bodies. The courts at every level are manned by lawyers. Many of the presidents have been lawyers—in this century alone, five out of 17, up to George Bush.

The American political system was devised by lawyers and is operated at every turn by lawyers who, among other things, have the most substantial immunities and privileges of any professional body of people in the United States.

Yet, as I have noted, anybody can be a lawyer, and often with relatively little effort. Some candidates for the bar, finding the requirements in certain states too stiff to negotiate, try for the bar in states with minimal requirements and later transfer their activities to high-requirement states that accept them without examination, as a matter of courtesy. While one may have some idea of what a "board certified" surgeon is, there is no comparable rating for lawyers.

The profession itself, however, knows who its top practitioners are and how to spot them. The leading law firms—that is, those with the most and largest corporate clients—like to pick those graduates of the ten leading law schools who have served on the editorial boards of the schools' law journals. These are regarded, rightly or wrongly, as the coming people of the profession and are paid extremely large starting salaries. Coming people are also those law-school graduates who are selected to be assistants to U.S. Supreme Court justices.

Others establish themselves as best they may, utilizing whatever family or school connections they may have. Whatever capabilities they may have they must, like most new workers, reveal in their performances. The law is a very crowded profession.

The poor public image of lawyers extends back for centuries. The term "crooked lawyer" is commonly heard. A general reason for this is that some litigants, defendants and patrons of lawyers, are emotionally upset by disappointment in losing cases or property claims and attribute their misfortune to underhand machinations either by their own or opposing lawyers. Lawyers, the fact is, are often caught in "no win" situations as far as earning public esteem.

This is not to say that some lawyers are not systematically and self-servingly unethical as opportunity offers. However, there is nothing about being a lawyer per se that induces dishonest behavior. The delinquent lawyer is merely a delinquent human being in an acquisitive environment. And if he is caught at some malpractice he can be punished.

With more than 600,000 people in the legal profession, many taken in with little formal examination of their bonafides, the law of probabilities concerning large numbers should apply to them. Hence, for every personal characteristic, half will be below a median point and half above. Each one, for each characteristic, will fall somewhere below the well-known bell-shaped curve on a chart, ranging from plus to minus. For every person in the legal profession who is there to stretch or bend the rules there is an equal number who are present to maintain the rules as rigidly as possible. This isn't to say that lawyers are not "flexible" but some are a lot less flexible than others.

Simply guided by the law of large numbers, the historical record and personal observation it seems to me that at least a quarter of the profession engaged in private practice in the United States is absolutely amoral, a law to themselves. Some of these are obvious shysters and pettifoggers but others, more dangerous, are harder to detect.

Miscreants among lawyers are often hard to detect and when they are detected are harder to bring to account. For the self-policing of the bar is pretty much of a myth. Complaints against lawyers are seldom pushed to final adjudication.

What happens to most complaints is illustrated in the following news item from the Chicago *Sun Times* of June 21, 1988, under the heading of COURT CLEARS 6 LAWYERS WHO LENT JUDGE MONEY:

"The state Supreme Court Monday refused to discipline six prominent Chicago lawyers for lending money to a judge—even though their actions violated ethical standards—because the lawyers didn't know they were doing wrong.

"The court said the lawyers were 'sailing in uncharted waters' when they lent money, ranging between $1,000 and $5,000 to Richard LeFevour, later convicted of Operation Greylord corruption charges.

"The disciplinary cases centered on a court rule that says, 'A lawyer shall not give or lend anything of value to a judge,' except for campaign contribution. [This last offers a revealing insight into the election of judges—F.L.]

"But the unanimous court said, 'They acted without the guidance of precedent or settled opinion, and there was, apparently, considerable belief among members of the bar that they had acted properly.'

"Cleared of impropriety were Philip H. Corboy, one of the nation's top personal injury lawyers; William Hart, a trial lawyer with close ties to the Cook County Democratic organization; defense lawyer Patrick Tuite, William Madler, and Samuel Banks.

"A seventh lawyer, Walter Ketchum, had his law license suspended for two years by the court for arranging some of the loans.

"Corboy, Hart, Maddux and Madler all lent $1,000 to LeFevour's dying mother in 1981. Tuite lent LeFevour $4,500 and Banks lent him $5,000 in the early 1980s."

So, in many ways lawyers are seen to lead privileged lives, which is perhaps fitting for these fundamental Guardians of the Republic. Like kings of old, they can seldom do wrong.

In any event, it is from the ranks of lawyers that judges, elected and appointed, are all chosen. At the time of their elevation they must all have established some sort of ascertainable record. At least until that time, however, they must never have been convicted of a crime.

V

THE STATES, in addition to politicizing the judiciary in the name of democracy, also came up with new democratic wrinkles. For many people were manifestly dissatisfied with the sort of government they were getting under the Constitution.

The new wrinkles came before the public under the names of Initiative, Referendum and Recall. All of these, like elections, are genuinely democratic activities.

The Referendum was first adopted by South Dakota in 1898, and until 1918 was adopted by 20 additional states in the following order: Utah, 1900; Oregon, 1902; Nevada, 1904; Montana, 1906; Oklahoma, 1907; Maine, Michigan and Missouri, 1908; Arkansas and Colorado, 1910; California, 1911; Arizona, New Mexico, Idaho, Nebraska, Ohio and Washington, 1912; North Dakota, 1914; Maryland, 1915; and Massachusetts, 1918.

The Referendum consists of a procedure under which petitions signed by a stipulated number of voters require that some law passed or proposed be submitted to a popular vote. The Referendum is initiated by voters. However, various state governments may submit new measures to popular vote. Massachusetts in 1780 submitted its first constitution to popular vote. Other states have used a referendum for constitutional amendments and for enacting new constitutions. And cities and counties have been allowed to hold local-option elections for liquor control. But the Referendum as a method readily available to popular initiative is restricted to the 21 named states.

The Initiative is related to the Referendum. It provides a method in which laws may be proposed by petition and submitted for enactment either to the legislature or to the people, or to both. It originated in Switzerland and is legal in 20 states, principally those named with the Referendum. Twelve states allow what is called the direct initiative and five the indirect, with three allowing both forms. But today every state except Delaware, Indiana and Rhode Island allows direct legislation by certain classes of cities.

The Recall involves, as the name suggests, the recall of elected officials—something of a reverse election or dis-election. It, too, is a Swiss device although it was used in the United States under the Articles of Confederation. Since then, it was first put to use by the city of Los Angeles in 1907. Oregon adopted the procedure in 1908 and then California (1911); in 1912, Arizona, Colorado, Idaho, Nevada and Washington took the same road, and thereafter Michigan (1913), Kansas and Louisiana (1914), North Dakota (1920) and Wisconsin (1926).

The state laws of recall variously stipulate they shall be applied to "every elective official," "every elective state and county officer," "every elective municipal officer" and so on. Idaho specifically excludes judges from recall but in other states judges may be subject to recall. Recall is not designed to replace impeachment or indictment for wrongdoing but is designed to enforce a policy at variance with one supported by an elected official.

All these methods are authentically democratic but the procedure of recall cannot remove a United States congressman. For the United States Constitution prescribes the methods of electing, qualifying, seating and expelling members of Congress. So no recall vote in any state could actually remove an elected United States official. Arizona, however, provides for the "advisory recall" of United States district judges, whatever that may be. None of these procedures applies to the national government.

The methods of referendum, initiative and recall may serve to indirectly intimidate recalcitrant state officials, possibly pushing them in undesirable directions as well as desirable ones, but they can have application only in state government. For the United States Constitution is, by definition, the supreme law of the land.

While there have occasionally been some spectacular uses of one or the other of these methods, in general they are little used because they are so cumbersome and create so much civil commotion. No electorate could make use of these methods steadily in the operation of government and still have much time for other affairs, like earning a living. They remain on the books more or less as a curiosity, except as a potential threat to incumbent officials, including judges who might be liable to make unwelcome decisions.

California voters in 1978 approved by a 65 percent majority "Proposition 13" to reduce property taxes in the state by 57 percent, thus sharply reducing municipal services that had been steadily built up by elected officials in catering to a variety of voting groups. Despite predictions of disaster, the state survived. Governors have from time to time been deposed by the recall, some later to be elected to the United States Senate.

Yet all of these democratic procedures—Initiative, Referendum and Recall—have largely fallen into disuse and there has been no serious attempt to incorporate them into United States Constitution which to date has kept the dervishes of democracy in harness, pointed presumably toward the light.

VI

WE SEE, then, that democracy involves at a minimum the general populace—The People—being closely connected with government decisions if not actually making them. This was the understanding of Madison and the Founding Fathers, and they felt the democratic principle was well expressed in the popular election for a two-year term of members of the House of Representatives. Some at the Constitutional Convention wanted the term to be for only one year so the incumbent could not grow away from the electorate; two years they felt to be too long. Others favored a term of three or four years but were voted down, so two years became the final length of term and remains so to this day.

It was in 1913 that the rising clamor for democracy (which, as we have seen, produced the Initiative, Referendum, and Recall) brought about the amendment to the Constitution that provided for the popular election of United States Senators. Since 1788, they had been elected by the respective state legislatures, but now that procedure was swept away in what was known as the Progressive Movement because it had been found that many legislatures elected senators after the legislatures had been thoroughly bribed.

However, the term of senators remained at six years, as

constitutionally provided, so that it was a long time before his constituency could review the work of a senator. By the time a senator's term has expired, whatever he has done in the Senate, whether reckoned as good or ill, is so extensive that most of his constituents have neither the time nor the attention-span to evaluate it all. Whether his constituents approve of him or not often depends on their general mood of the moment. Seeing nothing egregiously wrong in his performance and no attractive rival beckoning, the constituency re-elects him.

Students of elections have produced findings that show the incumbency itself is a powerful influence for re-election and many members of both houses of Congress and of the state legislatures find that they hold lifetime seats. It is too much trouble to find valid reasons for voting against an incumbent—that is, unless some dynamic and possibly unreasonable reason does surface.

The United States, then, does have elections, frequently, and up and down the line on Federal, state and local levels, including elections of most state judges. With the people presumably picking their representatives (if they really do), everybody, it seems, ought to be very happy. But many reports suggest that this is not so. Despite frequent elections there are many complaints.

There are Federal elections every two years. All members of the House of Representatives are up for election every two years along with one-third of the Senate. The founders of the Constitution liked such staggered elections because they felt the electorate lacked constancy as well as consistency. The founders, therefore, didn't want everybody elected at the same time, when the electorate might be in one of its flighty moods. The President of the United States is elected every four years at the same time as congressmen are elected.

But state, county and municipal elections are often held in the years when Federal elections don't take place. Thus American citizens in many places are offered elections every single year. Primaries come before general elections, so this makes for many elections. Some citizens see them as a surfeit. Many Americans, the fact is, are simply sick and tired of elections.

The lack of enthusiasm for voting in the United States is clearly shown in election statistics. Despite herculean efforts by both political parties, using every communications device including Hollywood techniques on television, voter participation, never very great, has been declining for many years. Beginning with 1960 and proceeding at four-year intervals (through the 1980 election) the percentage of voting age population who cast a ballot for President was 62.8, 61.9, 60.9, 55.2, 53.5, 52.6 and 53.1. The 1984 percentage shows that the winner, Ronald Reagan, won with slightly more than 25 percent of the eligible voters. In other words, just over one quarter of the eligible population determined who was to be President. The vote for members of the House of Representatives is always substantially less. In years when a President is being chosen, it is generally at least four percentage points less, suggesting that the voters are sending some sort of message. In so-called off-years, it is very substantially less and was 33.4 percent in 1986.

This is the reality, despite the fact, as disclosed here and there, non-citizens and illegal aliens are being allowed to vote. Come one, come all, is the voting policy in some districts. Voting by non-citizens goes back into the 19th century, when recent immigrants were freely voted by the local political machines in New York, Boston and other cities.

According to democratic ideology, people are anxious to vote if only to protect their freedoms. As long as voting is restricted to some, it is probably true that the franchise is wanted by those left out. But once the franchise is open to everybody, it appears to lose some of its charm, especially when it is seen that officeholders do not bring any particular boons to certain classes of people. The way to gain votes, politicians have discovered, is to buy them indirectly through expensive tax-supported programs. Such programs are designed to produce modern low-rent housing, low-cost or free food to low-income people, child-support to unmarried and abandoned mothers, general medical care for everybody, special educational programs for anyone falling below general norms and, in general, special support for all stragglers in the competitive battle of life.

Other politicians seek the votes of those who feel put at risk by the demands of the stragglers for greater tax support in order to equalize conditions of life for the stragglers. The resulting division is designated as one between liberalism and conservatism—the liberals wishing to be liberal with other people's money and the conservatives wishing to conserve what money they have.

The core of voters consists of government employees and their families. The employees alone totaled 16,690,000 in 1985, of which 81.9 percent were state and local. Allowing for only one more family member per employee, one has more than 33 million people, which amounts to approximately one-third of all voters. There is no legal obligation for government employees to vote, but on the state and local level, even where there is civil service, there is usually political pressure on employees to vote. This is true even of school teachers who, if they do not vote, run the risk of being considered unpatriotic. Furthermore, government employees today are heavily unionized and job-conscious.

All the large cities maintain party political machines that dispense many of the local governmental jobs, whether or not they are classified as civil service. Most of the rank-and-file party functionaries hold government jobs because on this level "Jobs" is the name of the game. And for this reason, in many cities and states the local elections are more important than the national as the local political machines have a decisive voice on the distribution of public jobs, including those of policemen, firemen and even teachers.

Laggardness about voting is not recent. Giving the franchise to women, as in 1920, and lowering voting age to 18, as in 1971, increased the numbers voting but not the proportions of participants. In 1932 in the Hoover-Roosevelt election, 52.4 percent of eligible citizens voted, approximately the same as in the Mondale-Reagan contest of 1984.

Little voting enthusiasm has been found among persons under 21 years of age. The reason unquestionably is that these young people have not yet had an opportunity to get their bearings in life. The age limit on voting was lowered owing to the fact that many critics pointed out that young men were eligible to be conscripted for military service but were not allowed to vote—a case of servitude without political rights. The anomaly might have been removed by excusing these youngsters from military service but instead it was removed by giving them the vote. Young women were included willy-nilly to achieve equality under the law.

Now any young man in the 18-21 age bracket can, if it is

proposed to restore conscription, vote against its sponsors. But his age group will be a small proportion of all voters who, under the proper stimuli, will presumably favor the conscription sponsors. The 18-21 group will have hardly any decisive influence on any vote.

Voting is purely optional under the American system of government. It is just as legal not to vote as to vote—take your choice. However, there are many people who make a great clamor about voting, holding that it is one's civic duty to vote. This is by no means certain, if at all tenable. Some of those urging one to vote have a pocketbook interest in doing so as they are in politics and believe the person being urged will vote their ticket. Another argument for voting is that the good citizen ought to vote to make sure that only good people get into office—as though good people had an unerring eye for good people. The fact of the matter is that no matter how virtuous, intelligent and informed a voter is, he usually has only a choice between two or at most three candidates for each office. And all the candidates are of a certain type of mentality, no matter what party they belong to or what program they espouse. Candidates in abundance of each of the major parties have shown themselves, time and time again, to be utterly deceptive in what they promise as compared with what they deliver.

One reason for double-talk by politicians in the United States is the heterogeneity of the people by every possible standard. There are not merely economic differences among people but regional, ethnic, religious, general cultural and educational differences. Virtually any direct, purely factual statement by any politician is almost certain to arouse angry responses from some quarter. So experienced politicians select their words carefully and speak ambiguously and elliptically.

Actually, from the point of view of the writers of the Constitution, popular voting is neither important nor, in fact, desirable. The populace at large, in the view of most of the Constitutional framers, should not even attempt to vote. The attitude of the framers is perfectly illustrated in the Constitution they wrote.

Popular voting for Federal offices was restricted to members of the House of Representatives. Here, as Madison said, was carried out "the democratic principle." But there was no popular vote for the Senate until 1913; each Senator, under the Constitution of 1787, was voted for by his own state legislature. According to Madison, what was fulfilled here was "the aristocratic principal." This thought was ventured, no doubt, on the presumption that only superior types sat in the state legislatures. Nor was there any popular vote contemplated for President. The President, according to the framers, was to be chosen by the Electoral College, the members of which would be chosen in such a manner as each state determined.

How the President was to be chosen is set forth plainly in Article II, sections 2 and 3 of the Constitution, as follows:

"Each State shall appoint, in such manner as the Legislature thereof may direct, a number of electors, equal to the whole number of Senators and Representatives to which the State may be entitled in the Congress; but no Senator or Representative, or person holding an office of trust or profit under the United States, shall be appointed an elector.

"The Congress may determine the time of choosing the electors, and the day on which they shall give their votes; which day shall be the same throughout the United States."

George Washington got the most votes in the first meeting of the Electoral College, with John Adams, leader of the original movement for independence, coming in second. Adams, under the rules, was therefore Vice President. At the next meeting of the Electoral College in 1792, the outcome was the same. But in 1800, there was a tie vote for Thomas Jefferson and Aaron Burr, the latter at the time a surprise upstart. When this situation was sorted out, with some resistance by Burr, Jefferson was declared President.

To avoid such a tie in the future the 12th Amendment was passed, calling for separate balloting for President and for Vice President.

The idea of the Electoral College, which was to act as a general buffer between either the people or the state legislatures and the Federal government, is generally regarded as one of the failures of the Constitution. The Electoral College survives today purely as a formality, with votes for President in all states being cast by the general citizenry in all their virtues and all their defects. This came about because, with the rise of parties in the states, notably Jefferson's Democratic-Republican Party, blocs formed in favor of certain known presidential candidates. Federalist electors had elected Washington and Adams but, in 1800, preponderantly Democratic-Republican electors elected Jefferson and Burr.

What the writers of the Constitution had planned was that the states would select non-partisan electors who would meet and canvass the nation for the outstanding public man of the day. And such men were, indeed, for a time chosen by the existing political groupings—Washington, Adams, Jefferson, Madison, James Monroe and John Quincy Adams. But the time was bound to come, as it did, when no particular man's name stood out. After Quincy Adams, the name most firmly in people's minds was that of Andrew Jackson, who had won the only American battle with Great Britain in the War of 1812.

After Jackson, most of the men chosen President were practically nonentities at the time of their election, except for Generals Ulysses S. Grant in 1868 and 1872 and Dwight D. Eisenhower in 1952 and 1956. All others, including Abraham Lincoln, were of so-so stature at the time of their first election. In point of prestige and stature, none of them, when first elected, had anything like the public standing of the first four Presidents.

Most American Presidents, when first elected, are very much synthetic creations of public relations experts, enigmas as far as their true character is concerned. It is only after they have served a term or two that people begin to understand them and then, in most cases, they are forcefully rejected. Franklin Delano Roosevelt, elected four times, is the big exception to this rule.

Most of the losers of presidential elections bear names unknown to the vast majority of the American public. Ask them to identify Horatio Seymour, Winfield S. Hancock or John Bell and they would be stumped. Presidential losers are, for the most part, headed for early oblivion, virtually unknown initially, and totally unknown after appearing briefly and then departing.

The writers of the Constitution had not anticipated (1) that a day would come when no outstanding personality would by his own character dominate the consciousness of the country and (2) that no political party would reach out to such a person if he indeed existed. What was really wanted by all parties in practical politics—the people who met the voters face-to-face—was someone, anyone, at the head of the ticket who would pull into office all of a party's lower echelons—senators, congressmen, governors, state office seekers and the myriad of others looking for some sort of government job.

From the viewpoint of professional party workers, the object of elections is to attain office and jobs. Consequently, whoever is perceived by the public as most attractive at a given moment is deemed most electable. And what counts most in a candidate with party workers is: what good will he do for the party faithful?

The Electoral College, instead of being a deliberative body as apparently planned, became simply an echo-chamber of a preceding public voting contest by white males.

In providing for an Electoral College, which survives as a useless appendage, the writers of the Constitution again showed their love of what they called "filtration" in the political process. While they wanted the existing government at all times to reflect popular sentiments broadly they sought to avoid, wherever they could, *direct* popular influence—except in the election of members of the House of Representatives. What they wanted was an interval of time before the will of the voters took effect.

But the clamor for "democracy" from the beginning proved to be too much even though popular voting under the Constitution simply did not eventuate in democracy but, under the Constitution, always in republican or representative government.

What we now need to do is scrutinize the more closely the idea of democracy as exemplified in elective government.

John Dewey, the noted American philosopher, was an ardent believer in democracy as is one of his leading interpreters, Professor Sidney Hook, for many years head of the department of philosophy of New York University. The article "Democracy" in *The Encyclopedia Americana* was written by Professor Hook and presents it in a very way different from that understood by James Madison and his associates of 1787.

Hook proposes a distinction between direct and indirect democracy in order, as he says, "to dissolve certain misconceptions." The first of these is "the view that the only genuine democracy is 'direct' democracy in which all citizens of the community are present and collectively pass on all legislation, as was practiced in ancient Athens or as is the case in a New England town meeting. From this point of view an indirect or representative democracy is not democracy but a constitutional republic or commonwealth." And this was the understanding of Madison and colleagues.

But, Hook says, "This distinction breaks down because, literally construed, there can be no direct democracy if laws are defined not only in terms of their adoption but also in terms of their execution."

This is Hook's novel factor—the execution of the laws under direct democracy. "For," he says, "delegation of authority is inescapable in any political assemblage unless all citizens are in continuous service at all times, not only legislating but executing the laws together. The basic question is whether the delegation of authority is reversible—controlled by those who delegated it."

Down through history, from the time of the Greeks, democracy related solely to making laws and policy, in which everybody participated, but not to the execution, which *necessarily* had to be done by delegates. The entire populace manifestly could not deliver the mail, police the streets, serve in the armed forces and carry on various other detailed chores of government. And it is clearly absurd to argue that the entire population, apart from setting policy, should be involved in executing in detail the laws and policies made by the entire population. In classical Greece, the democracy merely gave the orders for public servants to carry out.

The second misconception about democracy, observes Hook, is that it is frequently identified with or confused with the term "republic." "Strictly speaking," he feels, "a republican form of government is one in which the chief titular head of the government is not hereditary." But there are also non-hereditary kingdoms in history. A republic can have an undemocratic form of government, Hook contends, whereas a monarchy can be democratic, provided one accepts his indirect model. He cites Nazi Germany and the Soviet Union as such possible republics, although certainly the former is not classifiable as a republic. The Soviet Union, however, claims to be a federation of republics, but if it is, it is something completely unique in history. For as Cicero, a leading Roman lawyer, philosopher, public official and statesman, said pointedly: "Ubi tyrannus est, ibi plane est nulla res publica." ("Where there is a tyrant, there clearly is no republic.") And the Soviet Union has been the most thorough-going tyranny in human history.

Now, Romans as well as Greeks in authority certainly knew the meaning of their own political terms. They didn't need any latter-day commentators to tell how they applied. "Res publica" translates as "people's affair." For "res" is variously defined by Latinists as meaning "thing, object, matter, affair, circumstance." "Publica" means "belonging to the people, public, in the name of the people, at public expense." *Res publica* or *respublica* was used to refer to what in English is called "the State," which in pre-imperial Rome was the government elected by the male citizens. Under Greek democracy, the populace was regarded as making all decisions. Under the Latin republic, the elected officials made decisions.

As Hook writes, "There is no organic or logical connection between the two terms" although early Jeffersonians joined them in naming their Democratic-Republican party. This was taken to set the party adherents off against people who called themselves Federalists, whose leading men were the framers of the Constitution. And, to show the quirks of politics, one should know that the Federalists were not really federalists but called themselves that in order to attract to their side those who felt strongly about preserving the individual states, which functioned as part of a confederation—sovereign states confederated.

What the leading Federalists really were, were nationalizers and centralizers, out to subordinate the states and with the Constitution succeeded so doing. They were finally violently challenged on the battlefields of the Civil War in 1861. The writers of the Constitution ultimately and quite belatedly won their point—notably against Jefferson—with Lee's surrender at Appomattox.

The reason for all the seemingly futile word-play with terms like democracy and republic is their popular appeal. In reaching out and taking both terms for party use, the Jeffersonians were trying to develop a name with broader public appeal than that of federalism, and with the Democratic-Republican Party they succeeded. And, as time wore on and it was demonstrated that the term Democratic had more appeal than Republican, they dropped the latter.

It is for the same reason that politicians all over the world, including the leaders of one-party dictatorships, insist that their governments are democratic—indeed, more democratic than elected governments. They are more insistent on catering to the basic needs of the masses with measures like guaranteed (low-paying) jobs, guaranteed (low quality) housing and guaranteed free (rudimentary) medical service. For as the idea of equalizing benefits is applied, the benefits are necessarily diluted until they become insignificant in each individual case.

To their supporters the governments of the Soviet Union and its East European satellite states, along with Yugoslavia, Cuba, Nicaragua, Vietnam, Ethiopia, China, Angola and all other such centralized, one-party entities are more democratic than the governments of the United States and western Europe.

On neither side, however, does the populace really run the government. In the United States and western Europe, general public opinion has more influence than in the one-party dictatorial bloc where an artificial public opinion is generated by means of tight censorship. The big difference between the two types of government—one-party and multi-party—is the far greater amount of personal freedom permitted under multi-party regimes. There is little or no personal freedom under the one-party regimes. Furthermore, under the multi-party regimes there are operative protective constitutions while under the one-party regimes there are only paper constitutions that promise everything to everybody.

While people in the one-party states are under no illusion that they run the government, this illusion is widespread in multi-party states and especially in the United States. If one asks how people can believe such a palpable falsehood, one may also ask how millions can believe that they are destined to enjoy another existence after they die. In short, most people are able to believe anything they want to believe.

There is no doubt that there is an infinitely greater amount of individual freedom under the western governments than under the one-party dictatorships. But the western governments must all be constituted in rigidly stylized constitutional ways. And, once constituted, their fundamental authority is every bit as great as that of any dictatorship. The authority of all functioning governments is plenary. In other words, the ultimate order of a western-type "democratic" government is just as severe in its effect as the order of a Stalinist or Hitlerite government.

As illustration, one may look at the city of Yonkers, in New York. There, after proceedings dragging over many years, the United States courts determined that there was purposeful segregation of blacks and welfare recipients, contrary to law. To end the segregation, the courts ordered that the city build "scatter-site" public housing in place of concentrated high-rise public housing.

Virtually the entire city of middle-class suburban whites opposed this court order and a majority of their elected officials concurred. Despite the order, these men, in public appearances, argued that they had been elected to carry out the will of their constituents and they were doing this, which was just the opposite of what officeholders are often accused of doing: being faithless to their pre-election promises.

The city council appeared to believe that the "will of the people" was transcendent to a Federal court order, which was based on law that in turn was based on "reasons of state." In short, the elimination of segregation was necessary to the world policy of the United States, which in turn had in view the relations of this country to other countries.

What happened here was that the local democracy of Yonkers came into collision with the United States Constitution, and the democracy was squelched. Majority rule was repulsed. The situation here was similar to the clash that took place with respect to the Initiative, Referendum and Recall as it applied to Federal officials and laws. Democracy was repulsed.

Applying Hook's distinction, one would have to say that *direct* democracy was repulsed but *indirect* democracy, in the form of constitutional procedures, was triumphant. So to argue, however, is to bring out the fact that Hook's indirect democracy is a figment, a pleasant-sounding fiction. The argument in favor of indirect democracy would be forced to maintain that the constitutional structure was itself democratically devised, including all the rules that make amendment difficult—in other words, that democracy had erected a structure that would block majoritarian rule.

Rather than try to think one's way through such a maze, it seems simpler to recognize that the Constitution is a republican structure, as it claims to be, while the outside throng is part of the living democracy. This outside-living democracy, of course, can amend the Constitution whenever the legislatures or conventions of three-fourths of the states shall approve, a condition hard to meet by most proposals of constitutional change. By means of Article V, the framers first insured a considerable delay in effecting constitutional change and then required that a 75 percent majority of state legislatures or conventions favored it. At no time may the Constitution be amended by a popular plebiscite. All of which guarantees against any spur-of-the-moment constitutional changes. Direct democracy does not prevail and Hook's indirect democracy is trapped in a labyrinth of procedures through legislative bodies established according to rigid constitutional rules. Democracy, in other words, is harnessed, haltered and hobbled by the Constitution.

But even more decisive in showing where the decision lies was President Reagan's order of November 18, 1988, giving the federal government broad new authority to draft emergency evacuation plans for communities near nuclear power plants. For a long time, determined local opposition had confronted the never-powered-up nuclear reactor at Shoreham on Long Island and another plant at Seabrook, New Hampshire. Local and state politicians supported plant opponents. Under the law up to this point, community assent to evacuation plans had been necessary before a plant could begin operating.

Reagan's order swept away the requirement for community assent, although in the opinion of many observers, it came too late as other arrangements had been made with the concerned states for the disposition of the disputed plants.

The Presidential order, however, highlighted the fact that from the beginning of the Manhattan Project in the 1940s, no part of the nuclear development for peacetime uses had ever been submitted to public debate. Nuclear energy was in effect imposed onto the American economic system by the government. And in time, the public grew increasingly frightened of nuclear energy as it learned more about it.

If the American people can agree that they want to shut down all or any nuclear power plants, there is a way they can do it— pass an amendment to this effect to the Constitution. It is highly doubtful, however, that a sufficient majority could be obtained for this purpose.

But, compared with the populations of all the one-party dictatorships, who have no say whatever over their laws and constitution, American and western European citizens are as free as birds on the wing.

VII

A PRE-CONDITION for having a democracy that all philosphical democrats strongly insist upon, and which Hook endorses, is that the electorate must be well informed. And here we enter a highly debatable area since there are no certain methods for measuring how informed or educated a large population is.

One way is to develop statistics on the amount of schooling in the population, although schooling and education, though related, are very different things. According to Census Bureau data as of March 1986, for all members of the population 18 to 24 years of age, 21 percent had less than a full high school education, 44.7 percent had finished four years of high school, 27 percent had completed less than three years of college, and 7.2 percent had a college diploma.

College completions for those over 25 amounted to 19.4 percent for all ages, with some lowering of the percentage for those over age 55. But 25.3 percent of this population had not completed the high school level, while 38.4 percent had received high school diplomas and 16.9 percent had finished one to three years of college.

Increasingly, employers have been stressing the need for job applicants to have at least a high school education so as to be able to deal with ever more complicated instructions and printed directions. But a shocking number of instances have been found of utterly illiterate high school graduates who have been given disarmingly named "social promotions" by the schools. Standards throughout the American school system are uneven, trimmed to cater to a variety of constituencies. Many are solely interested in providing a diploma—which is taken to indicate a fully educated person. Throughout much of the school system, public and private, diplomas are freely granted to non-performers, and many school and college courses are a melange of both sense and nonsense.

The United States possesses some 2,500 four-year degree-granting colleges with enrollments of 600 or more persons, and about 1,000 two-year colleges offering what they call an "associate" degree. By this token, the United States would seem replete with educated people. Educational experts nationwide, however, almost totally agree that this is not the case and that the educational system is vastly uneven.

So complex is the American college situation that detailed guides to colleges are published, sort of an encyclopedic survey, compressed. Here various of the colleges are sorted out as selective, highly selective, specialized in various ways or left unrestricted—all code words indicating difficulties of qualifying for entrance. A vast number are easy to get into, requiring only, as it is said, a warm body and the requisite fees. Such, too, are usually liberal about granting degrees.

In view of this, where the formal education of a job applicant is deemed important by an employer, the custom has grown of not only considering the rating of the degree-granting college but also requiring a photo-transcript of a job-applicant's courses of study and grades. What courses a student completed and under what auspices may be considered significant. A Harvard diploma, contrary to common belief, may not be a passport to heaven on earth. For at Harvard, degrees are issued without commentary and *cum laude, magna cum laude* and *summa cum laude* (with praise, with great praise and with the highest praise). The latter are the ones that count with connoisseurs of degrees.

In general, technical schools like Massachusetts Institute of Technology and California Institute of Technology are more selective in accepting students and more rigorous in their programs than even the best of the liberal arts institutions.

Programs that de-emphasize mathematics, physical sciences, foreign languages, logic and semantics are favored by all the schools offering "soft" programs. For in the entire field of technologies, life and public safety are at stake. The fundamental criteria here are far more rigorous.

For this reason, government supervision of the programs that produce medical doctors, engineers and scientists is far more searching than it is for other educational programs. Most graduates in these fields are required to be publicly licensed before being allowed to practice. In every field, of course, individual initiative may push beyond routine academic requirements. Yet what experts see in American education generally is a bland dilution of the entire process so as to produce in the general populace an illusion of being educated—at least with a diploma to prove it.

The general striving for course credits as well as diplomas and degrees has led Robert Maynard Hutchins, one-time head of the University of Chicago and associate director of the Ford Foundation, to suggest that all new-born Americans be awarded a bachelor of arts degree as a birthright. This would satisfy the apparent public requirements and leave the quest for a genuine education to those willing to really exert themselves, thus separating shadow from substance. Yet it is probably educators who are most responsible for the public demand for diplomas because they have for years equated the diploma with earning power. This has been done even though the most successful moneymakers by and large have been meagerly educated men. One does not have to be much of an intellect to be a highly successful real-estate agent or stockbroker.

So, despite all the schools, colleges, universities, libraries, newspapers and magazines in the United States, and a horde of book publishers, there is great doubt among close observers that any large section of the American public is highly educated. *The New York Times* (September 4, 1988) reports that "1.5 million New Yorkers are functionally illiterate, with reading skills below the fifth-grade level. There are now at least 27 million Americans in the same predicament and the number grows by two million annually. Some are immigrants, but many more are students who left schools without learning the rudimentary skills." Neither did some who stayed in school!

Hook also emphasizes that in addition to being informed, citizens of a democracy must be active participants in governmental processes if the government is to be an effective democracy. But as we have seen in surveying simple voting statistics, such participation in the United States is at best tentative and tenuous.

The democratic citizen, it is commonly said, especially in the schools, should be thoroughly informed about his government. The chance of anyone being more than superficially informed, however, about anything as complex as the government of the United States is just about nil. Even the most erudite political scientists who devote all their time to the study of government know little of what goes on merely on the policy levels of the government until long after it is too late to do anything about it. If one could have a daily transcript of the significant proceedings on the government's policy level one could not find the time to keep up with reading it.

As for knowing what goes on outside the policy center of government, and in one's state government, any significant and continuing knowledge would be physically impossible to absorb.

From time to time Congress itself shows that it does not know what is taking place by launching elaborate and extensive investigations of some single phase of government activity.

After months of investigation and hearings, there are frequently spread on the record surprising revelations, often hard for citizens to believe.

So the idea of citizens being fully informed about what the government is doing is merely another nonsensical notion. The average American knows no more about what is going on within the United States government, even with issues of *The New York Times*, *Washington Post* and *Wall Street Journal* spread before him, than does the average citizen of the U.S.S.R. know about what the Soviet government is up to.

In short, what is called American democracy is more facade than solid structure, something like a Russian Potemkin Village. What there may be to it we shall see further along.

The usual argument about democracy is that it either is or is not desirable. The argument I am laying out is simply that it is non-existent, at least to any serious degree, and therefore not worth arguing about. Democracy in the United States is very much a fringe affair and were it not for the existence of the Constitution, it would long ago have destroyed itself. As it is, it has continued to live a shadowy, anemic and mainly rhetorical existence, thus serving, among other things, to obfuscate the political process and to befuddle the thinking of many people.

It is, therefore, the purpose of these pages not to suggest reforms of the political structure or process but simply to clarify what is taking place, to show where democracy begins and ends, and where—something entirely different—republican government begins.

VIII

POLITICIANS AND NEWS MEDIA commonly extol the wonders of democratic government which many Americans proclaim should be spread all around the world. This despite the fact that there are cultures that have endured for thousands of years without democracy and have brought their inhabitants down to the present, still survivors.

There is, in brief, an intense feeling of superiority in the United States and western Europe vis-a-vis the rest of the world, which is deemed backward, undeveloped. With development plus democracy, the rest of mankind might be brought into the economic heaven of the western world.

Democratic government, moreover, can be installed anywhere, it is thought—for example, in Central America, despite its possession of a largely illiterate peasant population. For all democratic government involves, in the opinion of its advocates, are elections within a multi-party system. Have those and something exquisitely good for everybody is certain to emerge.

But Central America alone is not a candidate for democracy. There is all of Africa, Asia and most of South America—always remembering that all there is to democracy (in the eyes of its boosters) is competing parties plus elections. And once one holds elections the result is—democratic government! It is all really very simple.

The process of elections works pretty much like a magic wand, eventuating in democratic government. And the government that ensues, according to Hook, is *indirect* democratic government. This is not the sort of government, to be sure,that the original democrats called for. Their slogan was not "Give Us indirect democracy."

The fact is, although thoroughly obscured in discussions about the American and European elective political systems, that there is a constitutionally constructed government system waiting to welcome aboard the newly elected members of the legislature and the new chief executive. In Britain and elsewhere in Europe, the elections are for Parliament, where a majority now selects the Prime Minister and the Cabinet.

To this, democrats of Hook's orientation argue that democracy has constructed the governmental system. And this contention is simply historically false. The United States Constitution was not produced under democratic auspices. What happened was that a group of men assembled to amend the Articles of Confederation in order to make them more effective, scrapped the entire project and then wrote a wholly new document. These men were sent to Philadelphia by the legislatures of the states.

The framers of the United States Constitution were not, as the record shows, enamored of democracy. They recognized its "principle" in permitting elections every two years to the House of Representatives. But, although they did not intend that the President be elected by "the people," the system they devised survived even though he in fact came to be elected by "the people." Moreover, the system still survived when in 1913 the public election of Senators was adopted. Popular elections did not alter the basic system.

The Federal Constitution survived, too, all the new elections at the state level, including the election of judges and the Initiative, Referendum and Recall. Elections, in and of themselves, are the solution for everything in the belief of democrats. But despite all this democratic surge around it, the procedures of the Constitution still prevail. Democracy ends where a Federal election ends, and at that point republican government takes over. And if the people in power can't make the restless public happy there are always the next elections to look forward to. These, however, often produce what is a case of "out of the frying pan and into the fire." As it turns out, there is indeed no Santa Claus—and no free lunch.

Whatever the result of any election, all procedures thereafter by the government are limited by the Constitution, which is interpreted by *unelected* judges.

The fact is, elections determine very little. They do not, for example, determine the policy of the administration those elections install in office. About this policy the public, and political pundits too, usually know little or nothing. Elections do not dictate governmental policy, which is often very much at variance with public expectations or diametrically opposed to it. In saying this, one is flatly denying the efficacy of democratic elections in determining policy.

At this point it is necessary to show in some detail that this is so—that the election returns decide one outcome and subsequent government actions have an outcome either greatly at variance or diametrically opposed to the electoral mandate.

IX

Let us begin with the national elections of 1912. In that year, the Democrats won the White House because the Republican Party split into two sections, one of which called itself the Progressive Party. An announced Democratic policy, in other words, did not bring about the Democratic victory.

From Woodrow Wilson's first administration emerged what most writers concede to be a triumph of many substantial reforms. There was only one cloud on the horizon, the European war, which broke out in August 1914. This war expanded into World War I.

The Wilson Administration at once announced a policy of neutrality and non-intervention. Britain and France, however, opened large credit accounts with Wall Street banks and their war orders gave a substantial boost to the American economy. Especially benefitted was U.S. employment, which had been sagging. This in turn enhanced the prospects for Wilson's second term, which heartened the Democrats who, except for the two Grover Cleveland terms, had been excluded from the White House (and much else) since 1860. The European war, in fact, was so much money in the bank for the Democratic Party.

By mid-1916, the combatants had stalemated each other in bloody trench warfare while high flying propanganda had been enlisted in a big way by the British and French to influence American public opinion. Nearly all of this propaganda, later investigation has shown, was false. But the end in view—to bring the United States into the war—was attained.

If in a war one side tries to kill the other, it is not worse to calumniate it, and Germany was thoroughly calumniated by Allied propaganda. Here the ground was being prepared for Hitler, whose forces actually committed unspeakable deeds of frightfulness in the knowledge that they would be falsely accused even if they behaved impeccably.

Germany repeatedly showed its lack of skill in international affairs (read: international viciousness) in which for centuries the British and French had been players. In the first place, Germany pridefully refused to seek credits in the United States at the outbreak of the war, which would have given her a staunch financial constituency such as the British and French automatically obtained. German pride was, optimistically, in her own power. It was *hubris*, which invited Nemesis.

Again, Germany repeatedly *announced* that she was going to do something frightful, thereby highlighting what was to come. The British and French merely did whatever they could think of that was frightful without trumpeting it to the world. Among other things, Germany announced she was going to begin unrestricted submarine warfare.

On May 7, 1915, the liner *Lusitania* was torpedoed off southern Ireland by submarine, with the loss of 128 American passengers. Germany had advertised that the ship carried munitions, and warned passengers away. This claim was denied by the shipping company although the United States knowingly had cleared the shipment. Only many years later was it established in a British court of inquiry that the ship in fact carried munitions and was a legitimate prey. At the same time, it was brought out that the Royal Navy knew submarines were operating in the *Lusitania's* path but, on orders from higher up, made no effort to intercept the raiders. It was brought out also in the hearings that the British government more or less wanted the *Lusitania* attacked because the attack would inflame American opinion against Germany. This it did.

President Wilson, nevertheless, adhered to his policy of non-intervention, and in the fall of 1916 was running for re-election under the slogan of "He Kept Us Out of War." In the meantime, however, unannounced preparations were being made to build up American armaments while the Wilson Administration was denying reports that it was planning to conscript men for the Army. In this and in many other ways it flatly lied, as Robert Nisbet reminds us in his surgical analysis *The Present Age* (1988).

And Wilson now swung from non-intervention to calls for "preparedness." Germany, meanwhile was being painted in more and more monstrous ways in the press, the same Germany with which the United States is now ultra-friendly.

Precisely in this period was born the technique of "The Big Lie," later made famous by the Nazis who adopted it and gloried in it. The "Big Lie," what could be called the atomic bomb of World War I, was developed by the French and British governments and was joined in devoutly by Washington. Lying was perhaps older than government in the history of the human race, a way of adjusting oneself in a situation unfavorable to one's plans, but "The Big Lie" was systematized with many ramifications. Above all, as the Nazis recognized, it compelled belief by its very incredibility. One such of many Nazi big lies was the asserted vast superiority of a mythical Aryan race, of which the Japanese were made "honorary" members! Germans, to be sure, were charter members.

The clergy joined in lustily with the anti-German propaganda of World War I, as reported by Ray H. Abrams in *Preachers Present Arms* (1933).

What Wilson did now with the declaration of war in April 1917, as the historian Page Smith puts it in his monumental study, was "to create a kind of supergovernment run by him through a series of commissions to which he gave extraordinary powers and which he usually backed when their chairman appealed for support."[1] Wilson's War Cabinet, composed of the heads of all the new war agencies plus the Secretaries of War, State, Navy and Treasury, was set up on the initiative of Herbert Hoover, at the time an experienced government official.[2]

The Wilson supergovernment consisted of numerous dic-

---

[1] *America Enters the World*, Vol. 7, p. 568, of *A People's History of the Progressive Era and World War I*, 1985.
[2] *Ibid.*, 572.

tatorial agencies presiding over all aspects of munitions, food, fuel, shipping, railways and trade in general. Under the War Cabinet was the War Industries Board, the National Railroad Administration, the War Finance Corporation, the Committee on Public Information, the Council of National Defense, the Federal Fuel Administration, the War Risk Insurance Bureau, the War Labor Board, the Aircraft Production Board and many others.

There was also a quasi-secret body known as "The Inquiry," which consisted of scholars on nations, ethnic groups, national boundaries and internal resources througout Europe.

At the same time, under George Creel at the head of the Committee on Public Information, there was begun an intense propaganda campaign against all things German—including German music back to Bach—and against any form of hyphe-nated Americanism. All things foreign suddenly were made abhorrent. Simultaneously there was unleashed a wholly uncon-stitutional reign of physical terror against any dissenters or "slackers" and especially against people with foreign-sounding names. Suspects abounded and informers sprang up all over.[3]

German-Americans had long been favorites in this country among all large immigration groups, with qualities most extolled by American moralists: hard-working, law-abiding, home-lov-ing, frugal, well-behaved, cleanly and friendly—in short, para-gons. Overnight they were transformed into dangerous fiends, potential spies, nasty saboteurs and general troublemakers, agents of Wilhelmstrasse. The teaching of the German language, once central to the high schools, was abruptly abolished, with Spanish and French replacing it. Phonograph recordings of Beethoven's music were publicly shattered. German-Americans by the thousands hastily Anglicized their names, from Weiss to White, Schwartz to Black and Baumgarten to Treegarden.

Much of what went on seems, historically, like a dress rehearsal for later more emphatic employment by Hitler's Nazis against Jews, Gypsies, dissidents and other captive peoples. And it was all unconstitutional, against the law on every level, a case of gross usurpation by the government, of government run mad.

George Creel accomplished wonders. As Page Smith writes,

---

[3] *Ibid.*, 540-66.

"The image of the United States as a land of freedom, justice, equality, and opportunity that had been so prominent in the decades following the formation of the Union and that had dimmed under the incubus of slavery and the land-grabbing war with Mexico and been renewed with the preservation of the Union and the freeing of the slaves, had been severely tarnished by the bitter war between capital and labor, by the aggressive imperialism of the nation in the closing years of the century, and by the well-publicized stories of municipal corruption in the country's major cities. At the time of the entry of the United States into the war its international reputation was at an all-time low.

"If the war did nothing else, it replaced that negative image—both internally and externally—with a brilliant, glowing picture of democracy's last and best hope. With all the negative elements, with all the doubts, criticisms and misgivings ruthlessly suppressed, the nation and the world were flooded with pro-American propaganda. Every familiar chord was struck not once but a thousand times. America the redeemer; America the pure in heart, the wise, the powerful, the benign, the particular vessel of the Almighty. Reams upon reams. We believed it with a great surge of hope and optimism, and so did much of the world, which needed desperately something to believe in."[4]

Creel's campaign was a model for the later-coming Joseph Paul Goebbels in Nazi Germany and has provided themes for American political demagoguery to this day.

All of which is set forth here as the foundation for a thesis I wish to express—to wit, no American national political campaign since 1916 is about issues a new administration intends to address; indeed, the incoming administration, like Wilson's, may go in the diametrically opposite direction to the one promised or implied to voters. A national election in the United States is never any more than pure theater, the side winning the election doing so merely because its themes impress more voters.

Where there is parliamentary government, the issues and the positions expressed during an election by the parties are likely to become the policy of the new administration. Under the Ameri-

---

[4] *Ibid.*, 578.

can system of government, there is no way that a new administration can be held to its election promises.

What the American electorate thought of Wilson was shown in the interim congressional elections of 1918. Wilson, head of a government which that same month had seen a victorious end to the great crusade against German bestiality, called for the election of a Democratic Congress "if you have approved of my leadership." He called, in effect, for a vote of confidence, a mandate. The electorate instead gave overwhelming majorities to the Republicans in both houses of Congress.

If the United States had a parliamentary form of government, Wilson would have been turned out of office on the spot, certainly an unusual outcome for the leader of a nation triumphant in a big war.

The Republicans won the election of 1920 under Warren G. Harding's slogan of "Back to Normalcy." It was not necessary for them to denounce Wilson's Fourteen Points or the Treaty of Versailles, which they did; the electorate was solely interested in rebuffing the Democrats and they did this again in 1924 and still again in 1928. While many pseudo-issues figured in all these campaigns, the excesses of the Wilson Administration largely affected the electorate.

By all signs, the Democrats were out of office forever and peace and prosperity seemed attached to the Republican Party.

The first crack in this prospect came in October 1929, with Black Friday and the stock market crash, the consequence of reckless speculation that had been financed by the big banks on thin equity margins. But contrary to long-standing belief, the ensuing Depression was not "caused" by the crash. In 1930, Congress passed and President Herbert Hoover signed the Smoot-Hawley Tariff Bill, giving the United States record high import tariffs. Foreign trading partners of the country retaliated in kind, with the result that international trade, and the manufacturing behind it, declined significantly.

In the same period, too, the Federal Reserve System kept interest rates high, which in the opinion of many leading economists had more to do with deepening the Depression than everything else. At the time, Federal Reserve interest rates for the nation were dictated by the Federal Reserve Bank of New York, which was run by the big Manhattan banks. One of

Roosevelt's subsequent New Deal reforms was to move the locus for setting interest rates to the Federal Reserve Board in Washington, where political considerations might more readily be brought to bear. Politics, too, may have influenced rate-setting when the Federal Reserve Bank of New York called the shots but these actions could be inimical to any national administration.

All these factors—the stock market crash, the raising of tariffs all around and the keeping of interest rates relatively high— helped worsen the Depression, leading to the unemployment of about a quarter of the labor force and part-time work for additional thousands upon thousands. The savings of many families were quickly exhausted, leaving many people completely without funds. This led to declines in consumer spending and further dampened production.

The presidential campaign of Franklin D. Roosevelt in 1932 barely mentioned all these matters although it stressed that "hard times" prevailed and blamed the Republicans, especially Herbert Hoover. The latter had in fact adopted many measures of relief but not direct aid for the jobless and penniless. At his appearance in newsreels in movie theaters, he was roundly hissed, unprecedented treatment for a President of the United States.

The Roosevelt campaign managers, like those in charge of the Harding campaign in 1920, knew they had certain victory. Therefore they were not moved to make any great promises to attain office. One theme their candidate stressed was overspending by the government, and he promised to halt it—a promise that was broken almost immediately after he took the oath of office. The balance of his campaign similarly touched on Democratic Party themes.

Nothing whatever was said about the New Deal deluge to come. We need not recount here the details of all the new agencies that were formed—known at the time as "alphabet soup" agencies owing to the bewildering array of initials composing them: NIRA, PWA, WPA and scores of others. While the press registered the surprise of many at all that was going on, regarding it as unprecedented, what the New Deal amounted to at bottom was nothing more than a resurrection of the Wilsonian special agencies. Only now they were not war agencies but were designated as emergency agencies.

What made the New Deal most popular was that it provided direct money relief to an army of pauperized citizens. The Public Works Administration financed a patchwork of projects all over the country, thereby producing employment and a demand for raw materials. The Works Progress Administration provided a large variety of make-shift jobs, such as cleaning streets and parks. But the general formula was that of creating new agencies.

While there were outcries that the programs were "communistic," in fact they had a strong rightward thrust, as exemplified in the National Industrial Recovery Act, or NRA, introduced with many street parades and much hoopla. What this act did was to cartelize the economic system of the country, industry-by-industry, very much along the lines of Mussolini's Fascist state. The NRA was enacted in June 1933, but in May 1935, it was declared to be unconstitutional by the United States Supreme Court unanimously.

The emergency the New Deal was coping with—unsuccessfully—was the Depression. Virtually all economists are agreed that what lifted America out of the Depression was the new war in Europe. This broke out in 1939 and led to the placing of war orders in the United States. The European war of 1939-45 assisted the Democratic Party once again as an earlier one had in 1914-16.

Roosevelt was reelected in 1940 and 1944, winning four successive elections, unprecedented and unmatched in American history. He is still regarded primarily as the savior of the common man. None of his campaigns, however, turned on any issues; the Democrats were always sure of getting the most votes by chastising Herbert Hoover, long gone from the public scene.

In 1948, the Republicans, for some reason sensing an easy victory, ran a lackluster campaign for Thomas E. Dewey. He was opposed by Harry S. Truman, who had succeeded to the presidency when Roosevelt died in April 1945. In effect, Truman served a full term as President, so he carried with him the aura of the incumbency.

The essence of Truman's campaign was to persuade voters to vote for him to protect the New Deal programs that had personally benefitted them. At the time, elements in both parties favored dismantling parts of the New Deal. Truman and his running mate, Alben Barkley of Kentucky, both made hundreds of speeches, many of them extemporaneous from the rear platforms of railroad trains on cross-country whistle stops, and denounced the 80th Congress as a "do-nothing" aggregation dominated by men with "a dangerous lust for power and privilege"—which one could say about virtually any latter-day Congress. Even though there were two aggressive upstart minority parties also in the field, Truman defeated Dewey by 24,105,812 votes to 21,970,065 and won 303 Electoral College votes against his opponent's 189. (All citations of election statistics in this text are taken from *The World Almanac.*)

There were, however, no concrete issues in the campaign. The winner in this, as in all issueless campaigns, entered the White House with a blank check. And decisions President Truman made, particularly with reference to foreign policy, had by no means been authorized by the electorate, either directly or by implication. In fact, most of what he did was a complete surprise to outsiders, and was so treated by the news media.

In order to prevent a general strike, Truman in 1950 sent in the Army to seize the nation's railroads, returning them to their owners in 1952. Emboldened by this success, Truman on April 8, 1952, ordered the seizure by the government of the nation's steel mills to avert a strike. The presidential order was ruled illegal on June 2 by the Supreme Court and was nullified.

Apart from retaining agencies of the New Deal, few if any of President Truman's actions followed the script of his election campaign, which is usual with all Presidents. The campaign and its themes have little to do with the administration that follows. All the election decides is the identity of the person who takes the oath of office on Inauguration Day. As of that day, everything that follows is more or less a mystery.

What elected Dwight D. Eisenhower in 1952 was nothing other than his overwhelming renown as the leader of the Allied forces in Europe against Hitler's *Wehrmacht*, compared with the relative obscurity of his erudite, witty Democratic opponent, Adlai E. Stevenson. Eisenhower's name had been on the front pages of the newspapers almost every day for more than ten years. He was a world champion and there was nothing threatening to anyone in his demeanor. The Democratic as well as the Republican Party each tried to recruit him. He was an affable, friendly man who seemed to merit his campaign slogan: "I Like Ike." And so in 1952 and again in 1956 Eisenhower beat Stevenson with crushing majorities.

In 1960, John F. Kennedy defeated Eisenhower's Vice President, Richard M. Nixon, by slightly more than 100,000 votes. There was some talk that the Kennedy forces had stolen the election with fictitious votes supplied by Mayor Richard Daley of Chicago. But an alteration of the vote for Illinois would not have cancelled Kennedy's lead in the Electoral College, where he won by 303 votes to 219. A redistribution of the popular vote would need to have been spread over several states to alter the Electoral College result, which was what counted.

This election, too, had no central issue but, as usual, it had a number of false mini-issues, these mainly supplied by the Democrats. One of these was that the Eisenhower Administration, led by a top military man, had allowed a "missile gap" to develop between the United States and the Soviet Union—that is, that the Soviet was ahead in the number of intercontinental ballistic missiles capable of carrying atomic warheads—a frightening thought to some voters. As it finally turned out, there was no missile gap, but by the time this became widely known, it was academic because the election was over.

Both Presidential candidates, however, declared resolute hostility to the Soviet Union in defense of world freedom. The essence of Kennedy's campaign was expressed in the slogan to "Get the Country Moving Again," although there was little evidence that it had stopped.

The Kennedy-Nixon contest brought out a record number of voters, nearly seven million more than in the election of 1956—a total of 68,335,642 votes for the two men. The reason for this sudden increase in voter participation was that Kennedy was a Catholic, the second ever to run for the presidency (Al Smith was the first in 1928). That fact brought out not only politically lethargic Catholics but also politically lethargic anti-Catholics.

Kennedy's decision to make a virtue of his Catholicism, to parade it in order to de-fang opponents who would use it anyhow in a whispering campaign, made him stand forth as a very religious man (which he was not), thus attracting many non-Catholics to his standard.

Religious considerations play a more or less great role in many

American national elections. Religious elements had much to do with Truman's surprise victory in 1948. For just about the entire Jewish vote went to him for the support he gave to the Zionist coup that established Israel in 1948, only a few months before the American elections. The Jewish vote alone could account for much of Truman's margin of victory over Dewey and two splinter party candidates.

The premise of Lyndon B. Johnson's victorious campaign of 1964 was a colossal lie, what Harry Truman called "a lollygaster." It was Johnson's claim in the election campaign that he stood for peace, was opposed to the expansion of war in Vietnam by the forces John Kennedy had sent there. It was his further claim, advanced by apparently detached elements, that his opponent, Barry Goldwater, was deranged. Goldwater had called frankly for a stronger crusade against the Vietnamese communists.

While Johnson was posturing as an apostle of peace and tranquility, he was secretly preparing to greatly enlarge the war, more or less emulating Woodrow Wilson's duplicitous role in 1916.

Furthermore, Johnson did expand the war and did it by means of false information or dis-information fed to the American people. He obtained a blank check from Congress for further action in Vietnam by means of the fictitious Tonkin Gulf "incident" in which American warships were supposed to have been fired upon by North Vietnamese torpedo boats. In the years that followed, no evidence was ever produced that such an incident ever took place. But Johnson had what he wanted, a mandate to enlarge United States forces in Southeast Asia at will.

Not only was Johnson a thorough liar but his lies brought to public view appropriate havoc at home in the form of riots and angry demonstrations by outraged citizens who were opposed to a pointless war.

Richard Nixon, no doubt emboldened by Johnson's success in bulldozing his way toward idiotic ends, achieved office by the false claim that he had a sure-fire plan to end the Vietnam War (which he continued for six more years), and while in office, deliberately broke just about every fundamental law in sight. Any law that stood in his way was simply broken by Nixon and his adjutants, most of whom wound up in jail.

Gerald Ford, a long-time member of the House of Representatives, was appointed Vice President by Nixon when Spiro Agnew was forced to resign while he pleaded *nolo contendere* (unwilling to contest) to formal charges that he had accepted bribes while he was governor of Maryland. Agnew is a duly proven criminal.

Until he resigned in August 1974, just prior to his impeachment trial, which would surely have led to his conviction, one word summarizes Nixon's two terms. That word is "Watergate," with respect to which there is a dense record of criminal machinations by his White House staff, including burglary and a very long string of street-level crimes for which other culprits served many years in prison.

In the course of the Watergate investigation, Nixon himself publicly announced "I am not a crook," although when all the evidence was laid out, it strongly indicated that he was a liar in so announcing. Nixon was pardoned, prior to any conviction, by his stooge, Gerald Ford, clearly showing that the system can be manipulated by top insiders. The only man in American history who was appointed Vice President and then succeeded to the Presidency by a unique accident, but was never elected to either post, Ford lost the election of 1976 to Jimmy Carter, former governor of Georgia, by 39,148,940 votes to 40,828,929, a narrow margin of victory.

Carter's campaign was one of those where the underlying issue really was the faults of the previous administration. Virtually unknown nationally, Carter won simply because he opposed the Republicans and Nixon's successor Gerald Ford, who himself has said that he believes he lost because of his untimely pardon for the disgraced Nixon. This could well be true in view of the closeness of the result, when a small number of votes either way could determine the outcome. Ford, to protect himself, should have delayed the pardon for Nixon until after election but he was apparently too obtuse to understand the politics of the situation he found himself in. One of the unusual points he had to contend with in the campaign was Carter's promise to the voters that, if elected, he would never lie to them. As an American presidential statement, this ranks with Nixon's claim not to be a crook.

But in the election of 1980, largely because of the perceived ineptitude of his administration, Carter was overwhelmed by

Ronald Reagan, Republican. The vote against him was 43,899,248 to 35,481,435 with 5,719,437 votes going to a splinter-party candidate, John B. Anderson. So the voting public was obviously very discontented with Carter. Anderson got only about six percent of the vote cast. In 1924, the 4,822,856 votes cast for Robert La Follette, the Progressive Party candidate, was more than 16 percent of the total cast. Third-party candidates rarely attract American voters.

Although the foregoing is the barest selective sketch of recent presidential elections, it is enough to sustain certain conclusions relevant to our theme concerning democracy.

The first conclusion is that the themes of the winning candidate in a presidential election do not predict the policy of the incoming administration. In short, the policies the voters think they are voting for are not the ones that are implemented, so that the voters really have nothing to say about what ensues. As the voters do not determine policies it can hardly be said that democracy prevails, even "indirectly."

If one approves of all the reform actions of the first Wilson Administration, as indeed do most political scientists, they are by and large policies never endorsed by a majority of the voters of 1912. However, they were devised according to the beliefs of the writers of the Constitution that the government is wiser than the populace and more likely to make the right moves. For a majority of the voters voted *against* the Democratic candidate, 7,699,942 to 6,286,214. But the non-Democratic Party vote was split between two candidates, who got 88 and 8 Electoral College votes each, while Wilson got 435 Electoral College votes and was, according to constitutional procedure, the winner. Here the Constitution, as in many other matters, determined the outcome, not "The People."

None of the achievements of the first Wilson Administration is, therefore, creditable to the majority of the populace, to the broad democracy outside the government toward which orators constantly point with fatuous pride. While the Wilson Administration was in essence republican, in that it took office according to constitutional rules, it was not something rooted in the populace, which had not ordered it according to democratic formula. If the opinion of leading political scientists is taken, the American public got better than it had voted for in the first Wilson Administration.

In 1916, Wilson won re-election by 9,129,606 votes to 8,538,221 for the Republican Charles Evans Hughes, a narrow margin of 591,385 votes or a little more than ¼ of one percent of the popular total. Out of this, Wilson got 277 Electoral College votes to 254 for Hughes, a majority by both counts.

Wilson won this scant majority not merely by his achievements in his first administration. For at the time the American public was very agitated by the European war, with many elements, responding to deceitful Allied propaganda, in favor of having the United States enter the war to punish the "militaristic" Germans and help the "democratic" British and French. For the Germans were clearly out to subjugate everybody while the British and French aimed to free everybody in an earthly paradise.

But the bulk of the populace, in the Midwest and Far West especially, was opposed to the United States entering the war, with many favoring Germany. The Wilson campaign tipped the balance with the slogan "He Kept Us Out of War," and its implied promise that he would continue on this course.

The Hughes forces at the time were perceived as favoring U.S. entry into the war. While hammering at the idea that Wilson had kept America out of the war, his administration simultaneously denied that it was preparing to introduce conscription or that it had decided to enter the war, in both cases a deliberate and colossal lie. It of course tipped the balance of the election although was not responsible for our entering the war because Hughes and the Republicans were clearly going in the same direction. Leading elements in both parties, especially among the big financial supporters, favored it.

So the broad American democracy was going to war no matter which candidate won. The voters had nothing to say about it, a strange state of affairs even if one accepts the idea of an "indirect democracy" at work.

This Wilson Administration imposed conscription, set up a string of wartime agencies on top of the existing government and began a reign of terror against dissidents. In theaters all over the country, lights would suddenly go on and government agents would demand of all young men in the audience evidence of their draft registration. Those who could not produce it were led away.

Conscription for service overseas was unprecedented in American history. All wars prior to the Civil War were fought with volunteers. The "democratic" South in the Civil War introduced conscription and the northern Unionists were forced to follow suit although any conscriptee could buy his way out of service for $300, a rather substantial sum for that time. But conscription for service thousands of miles overseas was entirely new then although it is now part of the U.S. system, albeit temporarily suspended. It can and will be introduced again if reasons of state seem to require it.

As Professor Nisbet points out in his book *The Present Age*, all the actions of the second Wilson term were totalitarian, designed to give the government control over every phase of American life. It was a blueprint, made in the U.S.A., of things later done in Italy by Mussolini and in Germany by Hitler.

Wilson's motto for promoting the war was: "A War to Make the World Safe for Democracy." In actuality, the war made the world safe for totalitarianism, first in the United States, then in Italy, then in Russia, then in Germany and Spain and elsewhere including Japan and China. With the ending of the war in 1918, Wilson's totalitarian structure was dismantled, but elsewhere, politicians having been taught a dazzling lesson, it flourished.

So with Woodrow Wilson the American democratic electorate got two administrations it never ordered—one that experts consider remarkably good and a second that an array of distinguished commentators consider an abomination. Wilson, it is true, has a considerable number of worshippers around. But so do Mussolini, Hitler, Franco, Stalin and Mao.

As I have indicated, the Republicans did not need to stage much of a campaign in 1920 as the electorate was thoroughly disenchanted with Wilson and the Democratic Party. It had shown this in 1918 when it swept into office a Republican Congress as Wilson pleaded for an endorsement of his policies. Wilson never got that from the electorate.

The Republicans won the election of 1920 and the next two by heavy majorities, landslides each year, so they had no need to practice any great deception on the electorate. They won in 1924 with Coolidge, too, despite the showing that there had been very great criminality in the Harding Administration, as exemplified in the Teapot Dome scandal. Albert B. Fall, Secretary of the

Interior, was sent to jail for accepting bribes to divert naval oil reserve lands to private oil companies, a presumptive dagger-thrust at the heart of America the Beautiful.

But by 1932, the electorate was mightily disaffected with the Republicans under Herbert Hoover owing to the enveloping Depression.

Except for those who were in it, the disaster of the Depression is hard to understand. For it was as though some silent and invisible enemy was slowly shutting off one's sustenance. This being a money economy, the broadening lack of funds simply cut people off from food, clothing and shelter. Many of those thrown out of work exhausted their savings. Others lacked funds to service mortgages on their homes, which were foreclosed. Still others were evicted for nonpayment of rent and the value of all rental properties rapidly fell. In some expensive apartment buildings in New York City, landlords allowed tenants to remain, rent-free, so that the buildings would not seem completely deserted, especially at night. Other landlords adopted the ruse of keeping lights on in empty apartments to give the appearance of occupancy.

Unreported theft greatly increased. In Manhattan, there were grocery store robberies (food as well as money) which were not reported by the media on the ground that reports would spread the break-ins, by giving people "ideas." Street vendors selling apples and other things to passersby proliferated and pan-handlers appeared in droves, popularizing the expression (and song) "Brother, can you spare a dime?"

Hoover took remedial steps by establishing a number of supportive agencies for economic and financial activity. But he did nothing to supply direct aid and so was perceived as unheeding and unsympathetic.

The Democrats, knowing that Hoover's goose was cooked, ran a low-key Democratic Party campaign against him in 1932. Among other things, the Democrats charged that the Republican Administration was profligate with money and promised to run the government more economically. Roosevelt won by a land-slide, 22,821,857 votes to 15,761,841, with 884,781 votes for Norman Thomas (Socialist).

Nothing whatever in the campaign foreshadowed the New Deal that was to come, which was something nobody in the electorate had ordered or expected. Here was another instance of a majority of the electorate getting more than they had even thought about.

What most endeared a majority of the public to Roosevelt, allowing his re-election three times, was the direct aid he supplied to a thoroughly frightened and bewildered populace. This aid took the form of direct welfare payments to incapacitated indigents, "make work" on the Works Progress Administration rolls for the able-bodied and widespread building projects for skilled construction people on the Public Works Administration. Public works were established all over the country, wherever localities requested such Federal bounty. Some localities took everything they could get, some were more frugal and some on principle took nothing.

The intent of the administration in all this low-level aid was to get money again into circulation, and this indeed it did, aiding the regular business system. At the same time, various structural reforms were made in the economy, investigations were launched and there was much denunciation of "economic royalists."

Roosevelt was widely seen as a populist to top all populists and was also seen by some as leaning toward communism, which was never the case.

In predicting Roosevelt's reelection in 1936, Al Smith, the losing Democratic presidential candidate in 1928, remarked, "Nobody shoots Santa Claus." And Roosevelt thereafter always won handily, with large majorities in the Electoral College vote.

Roosevelt's were the first administrations in American history wherein the "common people," the lower rank and file, felt they were being directly benefitted by the government. And in all his elections Roosevelt and his supporters invariably invoked the ghost of Herbert Hoover as their opponent. It was not necessary to make a reasonable electoral case. And Truman, as we have noted, won in 1948 by promising to retain all the New Deal "gains."

Had it not been for war orders toward the end of the 1930s the Depression might have lingered. As it was, war orders, plus U.S. rearmament and finally American involvement started the economy working again full blast.

But none of the events that took place under the New Deal had been previsioned or ordered by the electorate. For the electorate, it was a big surprise party, pleasant for most, intolerable to traditionalists, especially those who were lucky enough to have their heads above the financial waters.

Nor did the electorate prescribe or lay out the operating agenda of any of the administrations following the New Deal—the administrations of Truman, Eisenhower, Kennedy, Johnson, Nixon, Ford, Carter and Reagan. What actually happened in all these administrations was, as far as the electorate was concerned, largely a surprise—pleasant or unpleasant, according to particular tastes. For example, there was no suggestion during his campaign that Kennedy would send a large contingent of troops to Vietnam, misnamed as "advisers," or that Johnson was going to announce a "war against poverty" and extend various New Deal arrangements in quest of "The Great Society" or that Nixon was going to conduct himself as he did and, more especially, negotiate a rapprochement with "Red" China.

Whatever any administration is likely to do once it is installed in office is virtually a complete secret to those members of the electorate who vote it in. And sometimes it is a pleasant surprise to those who voted against it.

All of this clearly shows that the government acts independently of any cues from the electorate although at times it is willing to act on some of these cues. As of 1932, nobody would have predicted that the incoming Democratic administration would put on the books the Social Security Act and countless other New Deal measures.

In acting independently of the electorate's expressed wishes, as it often if not usually does, the government is doing what the Founding Fathers foresaw. They wanted the government to act independently and vigorously, saw little merit in democracy, and had nothing to do with various democratic features added to the electoral system such as popular voting for the senate, giving the ballot to women and lowering the voting age to 18 years.

These added features have not greatly altered the governmental system other than to promote deception by incumbents and aspirants to office. But although the populace now votes for all officers (except judges), and for the President too, the expectations of a majority of the electorate are often frustrated. It can therefore not be said that the government is acting in obedience to a voting mandate.

X

A GREAT DEAL that goes on in the American government is secret. And quite often illegal. The same state of affairs presumably exists in other so-called democratic governments.

The electorate has obviously not prescribed this secret activity, along the lines of what was shown in the Watergate investigation. And it has surely not ordered anything illegal—that is, unconstitutional. So we here come to another level in which the popular vote has no influence whatever, where democracy is clearly not in evidence.

The government has openly, and with the concurrence of Congress, provided for a limited amount of secret "in the national interest" activity directed at clearly announced enemies of the United States, such as the Soviet Union under Stalin and his successors in the period after World War II. Such secret activity is the province of the Central Intelligence Agency, which from the beginning, in view of the evident menace of the Soviet, met with open public approval. There is, too, secret activity against criminals, which is also legal and publicly approved.

But much of this allowable secret activity, many investigations have shown, has been directed to other and quite illegal ends, and some of it directly against the populace itself—an instance of the government attacking its own theoretical foundation, "The People," like an old-style autocracy. Whatever else this may be it is surely not an example of democracy.

In main, illustration of what I refer to is the fact that much that the C.I.A. has done, both at home and abroad, has had nothing to do with communism or the Soviet Union. It instead had private ends in view of interest to the administration in office.

Case #1 relates to Iran. There, after World War II, the government was approached by western oil companies in a quest for drilling concessions. But in 1951 the Iranian Majlis (Parliament) passed a law nationalizing the petroleum industry, which it had a sovereign right to do. In the same postwar period, Great Britain, for example, had nationalized many entire industries. The Majlis then named Mohammed Mossadegh premier, empowering him to form a government to nationalize the Anglo-Iranian Oil Company, which had operated on the scene prior to the war. What the Iranian government was after was a larger share of the profits of drilling for and refining oil; these profits had formerly been divided between the company and the government.

As British technicians were deported, the United States now put itself forward to deal with the impasse. Failing to move the Mossadegh government, the United States mobilized, by means of money, secret forces under command of the C.I.A. operatives. These forces toppled the Mossadegh government and elevated Shah Mohammed Reza Pahlevi from subordinate status to supreme authority. Martial law was declared and Mossadegh and his lieutenants were tried, convicted and jailed.

The excuse given for the action against Mossadegh was that a Communist coup was imminent. This claim has since been shown to be false. There were, indeed, Communists on the scene, but they were all over, in small numbers, even in the United States.

This action by the C.I.A. was without a shadow of constitutional support. And far from being an independent body, the agency is under the direct authority of the President. It, and the F.B.I., which is also often spoken of as though it was something autonomous, is as much a direct instrument of the President as a concert piano under the fingers of Vladimir Horowitz.

The overthrow of Mossadegh's government was not only

illegal and undemocratic but was also against the precepts of orderly republican government. Under the theory of indirect democracy, which as we have shown is a mirage, the government acts under authority delegated by the electorate. But in Iran a government agency acted far beyond any delegated power. It literally usurped power and gained for the United States the hatred of an ancient nation that preceded it on the stage of world history by more than 2,000 years. While it is no doubt true that most Americans think of Iran as a place of no consequence, this is only because of popular ignorance.

The Shah, once installed, proceeded to install a thoroughly vicious, repressive dictatorship that ruled by means of torture and secret police, the latter organized by the C.I.A. The Shah was a puppet of the United States government and controlled by the C.I.A. An oil agreement—the object of all the strategy—was now negotiated with a consortium of eight companies, one of which was British and held 40 percent of the stock, plus five American, one Dutch, one French. Ultimately there were 17 companies in the consortium. But, one should notice, British exclusivity, which had once prevailed in Iran, was now broken in recognition of Great Britain's diminished power in the world. The big new intruder was the United States, along with its companies.

Case #2, Guatemala. The government of Colonel Jacobo Arbenz Guzman was overthrown in 1954 by a force directed and paid for by the C.I.A., as freely reported in newspapers of the day. The excuse for knocking out the Arbenz government was that it was Communist-oriented and the United States and its people were, as was well known, opposed to communism. And, the known fact is, the weak local Communist Party did indeed support the Arbenz program as the Communist Party, where it was not in power, supported one or the other of the traditional parties. In the United States, the Communist Party from 1934 to 1945, with the exception of the brief interlude of the Hitler-Stalin pact, was a strong backer of Franklin D. Roosevelt, the Democratic Party of the United States and the New Deal.

Therefore, one could reason, if support from a Communist Party justifies the overthrow of a government then Roosevelt and the New Deal were legitimate targets for a violent overthrow. It follows that since there was no attempt to overthrow it by violent means, the American populace was not only gutless but faithless to its political beliefs. Or ignorant of the situation.

Although the Guatemalan government, which since 1970 has been a harsh dictatorship toadying to the United States, was not Communist at the time, any more than the New Deal was, it was, according to the *Enclyclopedia Americana* (edition of 1971), "determined to limit the influence of the interlocking U. S. corporate structure operating in Guatemala—the United Fruit Company, International Railroads of Central America, and 'Empresa Electrica' (a subsidiary of Electric Bond and Share Company). This brought it into sharp conflict with the entrenched economic interests. At the same time, its efforts at mass mobilization and social revolution through a substantial program of agrarian reform disturbed the military. The result was a United States-supported exile invasion from Honduras." (See article, "Guatemala," Vol. 13.)

What the agrarian reform consisted of was the nationalization of millions of acres of corporate-held land, most of it owned by the United Fruit Company of Boston. This company had direct connections to John Foster Dulles, the American Secretary of State, and his brother Allen Dulles, Director of the Central Intelligence Agency, and it was these two men who set into motion the plot to destroy the Arbenz government.

Arbenz, one should note, was duly elected in free elections in which he promised the voters that he would nationalize foreign-held land and distribute it to the peasantry. In Guatemala, as in Iran, the issue was not communism but nationalization of an industry, as in Great Britain in the same period.

If nationalizing an industry is wicked, then Great Britain is wicked. But can Great Britain, our great friend abroad, be wicked? This is clearly impossible, so a double standard must be at work: what is wicked for some countries is not wicked for others.

Case #3, Chile. The government of that South American nation, duly elected, as per democratic prescription, was overthrown in September 1973, with the assistance of the C.I.A., with the Chilean military bearing the front-line burden. In the process, President Salvador Allende Gossens, elected in 1970 by one-third of the participating voters, was killed. Allende was an avowed Socialist of Marxist orientation but it was not this that aroused the ire of the United States, which for years had enjoyed friendly relations with Communist Yugoslavia and was in this same interval effecting a friendly rapprochement with Communist China.

It is, in fact, *never* Marxism, communism, socialism or anything ideological whatever that impels the U. S. government to "destabilize" a foreign government. What mostly arouses ire is nationalization of properties held by American companies. This was true in Chile, where the substance at issue was copper. Chile contains the world's largest known copper reserves and is also rich in other minerals, all of which were being exploited by foreign companies, notably the Anaconda Copper Mining Company of the United States.

What of the fact that it was foreigners who had ownership of these properties? How did they get these? In all cases they obtained concessions from earlier governments by means of bribery and allocations of partnership in the new enterprises. In no cases whatever were the concessions granted by fairly elected republican or democratic governments. The deals were always *sub rosa*, under the table.

Case #4, Nicaragua. For most of this century, Nicaragua has been one of the informal fiefdoms of the United States abroad, under presidents of both major parties. If blame attaches to anyone for Nicaragua, or for American adventures in Iran, Guatemala or Chile (or other similar places), it is shared by both parties. So any fingerpointing of one party against the other, especially in Congress, is so much hypocrisy.

Off and on, Nicaragua has been occupied by United States Marines, for the last period between 1926 and 1933. Prior to that period, from 1912 onward, the United States had on the ground as a legation guard a detachment of about 100 marines. Nicaragua, about the size of Iowa, has had a turbulent history. From the time of its independence from Spain, in 1821, to the present, internal strife has been continuous. From 1826 until now, the country has had 14 constitutions.

In January 1937, Nicaragua was taken over by General Anastasio Somoza, commander of his country's National Guard. A dictator, he ruled as a United States puppet until he was assassinated in 1956. He was quickly succeeded by his son, Luis Somoza Debayle, who like his father was a vicious, self-aggrandizing dictator until he was deposed in 1979. Those who deposed him called themselves Sandinistas, in honor of Augusto Ceśar Sandino, a past guerrilla leader (assassinated in 1934) who had refused to bend to U. S. rule.

A split ensued in the Sandinista movement, in part because its leaders balked at holding elections, which would throw open the offices to anyone who could get the most votes. The core of Sandinistas turned out to be Marxists, who soon received huge amounts of military aid from the Soviet Union. At the time, the Soviets clearly thought to turn Nicaragua into another Cuba, at least a thorn in the side of the U. S.

Dissidents, known as "Contras," took to the back country and fought the Sandinistas. They were voted $100 million of support by the U. S. Congress as recently as 1986, and President Ronald Reagan, without the approval of Congress, arranged to fund them by constitutionally questionable methods. Blame directed at Reagan by Congressional Democrats for conditions in Nicaragua, however, is wholly hypocritical as the Democrats controlled all branches of the U. S. government throughout most of the rule of the Somozas, who, one could truthfully say, were the instruments largely of Democratic Presidents—Roosevelt, Truman, Kennedy, Johnson and Carter. True, Republican Presidents in their turn collaborated.

But to say the trouble in Nicaragua stems from lack of elections is to simplify idiotically. For Nicaragua and many places similarly controlled are not capable of holding even fairly reasonably staged elections. The electoral process is apparently as baffling to people of strange cultures as a foreign language would be to uninstructed Americans.

Presidents of both major parties have accepted these arrangements with subordinate foreign countries, regardless of who was in the White House when the process started. As a consequence, the United States has long had a motley procession of dictatorial foreign puppets under its thumb: the Shah, the dictators of Central America, Pinochet in Chile, Batista in Cuba before Castro, Marcos in the Philippines and a variety of others.

While news of some of this turbulence is conveyed in the news media, most Americans know little about the close connection of their government with the events. Usually their government is presented in the media as a rescuer on the scene. But at intervals members of the party that is out of national office never hesitate to accuse the White House of gross and even murderous wrongdoing. How can this be? What is it all about?

In all these foreign embroilments it will be noticed that it is always the President who is acting, sometimes through one of his handy agencies like the C.I.A. If not that, then it is the State Department.

It is the Constitution that, in vague language, places the President in charge of U. S. foreign policy. He formulates it or, after conferring at his pleasure with others, conveys it. And he executes it. The President, says the Constitution, "shall have the power, by and with the advice and consent of the Senate, to make treaties... he shall... appoint ambassadors... and consuls... he shall receive ambassadors and other public ministers." The President, in short, is the only elected official authorized to have contact with foreign countries and their representatives.

As there is no precise definition of what the President may do, or limitation upon it, it follows that he may make any arrangement whatever outside the United States unless blocked by some other power, legislative or judiciary. It follows that he may destabilize or subvert existing governments abroad, that he may do practically anything. Abroad, a President of the United States is a powerful dictator.

While the Constitution does impose certain limits on a President with respect to the United States itself, there are no such limits upon him for actions outside the United States. And few of the actual limits on him are such that, history shows, he cannot frustrate. A President of the United States has much more scope for individual action than does, for example, a British Prime Minister, who must always report back and confer with the cabinet. He may also be questioned directly in Parliament. All of which is something that few Americans understand, especially those who believe they live in a democracy and under a democracy.

In making foreign policy, what a President does is meet the ambassadors of existing governments and reach mutually satisfactory ways of agreement. But in countries where turbulent political and social situations exist, he may do anything at all. In some cases he may merely withdraw. But in other cases, where American lives or property are at stake, he may take any action at all suitable to the occasion, without consulting Congress. Again, as to what the situation is that he is dealing with, he may report it truthfully, guardedly or falsely. In short, he may lie, and with impunity. Political opponents may denounce or criticize him for what he has done but he is not answerable for what is taking place as it is not taking place in the United States.

What he is doing, whatever it is, is wholly within the Constitution, especially if it is being done by puppets established and recognized by him as spokesmen for a government. For they are not his acts although he may be supporting the actors with his forces, paid for with American funds. But—and I here come to the vital point—what he is doing is in no way to be construed as democratic. His actions in these situtations are constitutional but hardly democratic even if he has been democratically elected.

Nor is a President faithless to his oath of office for supporting and underwriting foreign puppets. All any President is required to do upon being elected is to swear to uphold the Constitution of the United States (as interpreted by the Supreme Court). He is not required to act democratically, more especially outside the United States. Hence the procession of dictatorial American puppets one finds scattered from time to time all around the world.

In no case does any of this involve constitutional wrongdoing by a President although the outcome in no case conforms to democratic precepts. After all, it is also hardly democratic when American troops, far from home and on foreign soil, engage in combat with natives.

Beyond this, a President may too, quite constitutionally, intervene with a puppet against the puppet of another large foreign power, and thus promote warfare with no declaration of war by Congress since no American troops are, theoretically, involved. This, for example, was done in Angola where Moscow-assisted Communists had established a government that was supported by Moscow-financed and Moscow-transported Cuban troops. The United States, through the President, came to the assistance of a local rebel, Jonas Savimba, and helped finance and supply his forces. Savimba was even invited to the United States and received in Washington.

The President, events have shown, can thus intervene surreptitiously in any war, without the assistance of Congress, as President Roosevelt did in aiding Britain during World War II before the Axis powers had declared war on the United States (or we on them). In attacking the United States, they acknowledged that we were their secret foe, a staunch friend of Great Britain.

In acting as he does abroad, the President, in every case, is acting in defense, as he sees it, of Americans and American interests. The main point is that only he has to so see the situation. He has no need or obligation to discuss it with outsiders. He is, in the indicated foreign area, and under the Constitution, very much of a dictator. The forces that go down under pressure of the forces he puts into the field go down by his decree. It was a mere presidential decree that dethroned Mossadegh in Iran, Arbenz in Guatemala and Allende in Chile.

And when a President grows disaffected with some local dictator he has been supporting, that dictator seems to disintegrate, as was the case with Batista in Cuba, Trujillo in the Dominican Republic and Marcos in the Philippines. In many cases, as with Marcos, it seems it is enough that the word be passed along some secret channel that the leader is in the American presidential doghouse for a strong opposition to develop. Naturally, plenty of local people always hate the dictator because of his many merciless acts.

I have by no means cited all the cases of record in illustration of my point, just a few. The list could be greatly extended. What the President is doing when he intervenes abroad is not primarily restoring law and order but protecting American interests—as he alone sees them. This is constitutional and in accordance with his oath of office. The President, it may be remarked, is under no constitutional obligation to bring democracy to the world.

XI

IN NONE of the preceding matters or in any like them were the expressed wishes of American voters in any election carried out. While all these events were impending—in Iran, Guatemala, Chile, Angola and elsewhere—the electorate did not know about them so they had no chance to approve or disapprove. And when it knew of the events, the populace was given false information about the reasons for the action—that it was to combat communism.

It was not told that the issue was not communism but was nationalization of specific foreign-held properties. The electorate, in other words, was not properly informed so could not, even if it had wished, make an intelligent democratic decision about it.

In brief, in no way was democracy in action. Nor could it be, as the United States is not a democracy but is a republic, run by men who are given independent power by the Constitution. For while sections of the public from time to time want the government to do certain things, these sections and the entire electorate in fact have no way of forcing the government they have elected to do certain things.

When push comes to shove, the United States Government is as independent of the populace as is any government, including the Soviet Government. The main difference—and it is a big one—is that the members of the government, in a relatively short interval, will have to come before the electorate for a review of their actions. But at that time, the electorate will have hundreds of things to think about, including its own economic stability.

But, many investigations have shown, the United States Government, at the behest of Presidents, has taken high-handed, unconstitutional and illegal actions against large numbers of American citizens at home. This sort of thing began with the second Wilson Administration, when the government went hogwild in repressive actions against its own citizens who were doing nothing illegal.

And it is well to remember in discussing all such matters that they were never mandated by the electorate, either in or outside an election.

In the second Wilson Administration, the government, under the direction of Attorney General A. Mitchell Palmer, arrested a large variety of citizens and aliens on the ground that they were "radicals" and were in disagreement with the government about the nature of the war then going on. Many were summarily deported. Others were harassed, some for being insufficiently enthusiastic about the war or for being pro-German. A large part of the heavy electoral majorities attained by the Republicans in 1920, 1924 and 1928 were from German-American voters.

As of 1980, a total of 50 million Americans considered themselves of English or part-English ancestry, more than 49 million of German or part-German ancestry and 40 million of Irish or part-Irish ancestry.[1] To attack any identifiable large voting group is politically suicidal, yet this is what the Democrats did under Wilson.

It took the Depression to make a majority of voters switch allegiance from the Republicans to the Democrats in 1932. The politically-inept Herbert Hoover was blamed for the Depression. In a way, this was poetic justice as Hoover had been elected in 1928 as an apostle of evergrowing American prosperity, a chicken in every pot and two cars in every home garage. The Democrats were now to control the government.

The next big frontal attack against an ethnic group was the

---

[1]*Ancestry of the Population by State*; 1980, U. S. Bureau of Census, pp. 1-2.

roundup of all Japanese and Japanese-Americans following the bombing of Pearl Harbor. Here, with the concurrence of all branches of the government, including the highest courts, 110,000 Japanese, including 75,000 U.S. citizens, had their property confiscated and were moved into concentration camps in the United States for the duration of the war on the ground that, as with German-Americans in 1917 and 1918, they might be saboteurs or spies. (No German-Americans or Italian-Americans were so treated at the time.) As it turned out, not a single offender among the Japanese was found even though the U.S., as a military conqueror, had full access to Japanese records in Japan. The Japanese were completely innocent. Many, in fact, served honorably and heroically in the United States Army in the war in Europe. In this instance, the United States in 1988 acknowledged its fault and agreed to compensate the surviving Japanese with a payment of $20,000 each.

It isn't often that any government formally confesses to fault so this act of contrition should not go unnoticed. At the same time it serves to guarantee the truth of the charges of reckless highhandedness against the Japanese.

But the government does not act inimically only toward specific groups. It also does so at various times against the general populace, against the ostensible agents of democracy. In short, the alleged presence of democracy does not serve to control the government in the interests of the people.

This has been seen from the beginning in the policy of secrecy with respect to atomic energy. From the beginning with the wartime Manhattan Project, all matters atomic have been cloaked in the heaviest possible secrecy—although agents of the Soviet Union almost from the start penetrated all security measures. Secrecy was understandable for a strategic weapon like this during the war, but that secrecy has continued with respect both to military and industrial uses of atomic energy, resulting in harm and even premature death to great numbers of people.

The excuse for much of this secrecy is that the government did not wish to unduly alarm the populace, that it had to make a "trade off" in the interests of national defense. I do not fault the government here for this decision but I do stress that it was not a democratic decision, even indirectly. The public is rightly alert to avoid dangers, and when it comes to choosing among the dangers to be avoided, the public will choose to avoid the one that is nearer in time and place. As between the danger of being conquered by the Soviet Union, or attacked by it, and the danger of being harmed by nearby atomic emanations, the last is felt to be the more immediate danger and the one most people would choose to avoid, even at the expense of giving the Soviet Union some advantage. But the government chose to go opposite to this view, which only shows that the decision was hardly democratic, either directly or indirectly.

From the very beginning everything about atomic energy was veiled as much as possible from the public. This can be said even though, also from the beginning, general explanations of its nature were quickly available. But nothing was available about any atomic-power activity in one's near neighborhood. People lived near all atomic-energy installations and were not aware they were exposed to any risks. And were not warned.

The government made repeated tests of atomic explosions at its Nevada testing grounds, in some, exposing troops in near proximity to the blasts. All such above-ground explosions sent into the air clouds of radioactive dusts that drifted eastward over adjacent Utah. These clouds would tend to settle over certain areas and there were partly alarmed calls for information about the possible dangers. Demands for information became clamorous and President Eisenhower is on record as having told his aides to answer the questions ambiguously, without admitting there was any danger. As the scientists involved all knew, there was lethal danger. But the residents of Utah who were affected were not told this.

And, in the outcome, what has been positively shown is that there has been a high incidence, far above ordinary statistical expectations, of cancer deaths in the areas where the atomic clouds of dust settled.

I don't want anyone to think I'm pointing the finger at President Eisenhower uniquely. For I believe he was a more trustworthy man in the White House than any of those who have followed him to date; he did only what he felt was required. My point is that what he did was not prescribed by the populace and would not have been prescribed had they known.

From the very beginning, the dangers of atomic energy were

screened as much as possible from the public and the entire atomic energy industry was funded and launched with a minimum of discussion, as though it were a mere case of a new fuel having been discovered. Atomic-powered electricity-generating plants were constructed around the country until they now supply about 20 percent of all electric power.

As to the possible dangers, proponents of atomic power point out that the burning of wood, coal or oil also poses dangers to everybody living downwind. This is true but the dangers are much more diffuse, are thinned out and are spread over wide areas. Cumulatively they may affect some who are rooted to a certain location but these days most people move about a good deal, so diffuseness plus mobility of potential victims reduces the hazards. With atomic power, however, the danger from a single mishap or test explosion can be fatal to many people, as proven in the 1986 Chernobyl disaster.

And just how extensively surrounding areas have been endangered by unannounced atomic leakages is not known. It was disclosed by the nation's press on November 4, 1988, that the Department of Energy and its predecessor, the Atomic Energy Commission, had kept secret for 28 years a number of serious reactor accidents at the Savannah River Plant in South Carolina. According to *The New York Times* of this date, "The Energy Department said the failure to disclose the problems illustrated a deeply rooted institutional practice, dating from the first days of the Manhattan Project in 1942, which regarded outside disclosure of any incident at a nuclear weapon production plant as harmful to national security."

The excuse here was that the Soviet Union, an inimical power, would get to know. And by all indications, the Soviet Union all along knew as much about atomic power as the U. S. did. It is a constant American belief that people abroad are less informed than are Americans. Yet the whole of atomic knowledge was brought to this country by foreigners, refugee scientists from Nazism and Fascism. All the U. S. contributed was the financing for a vast amount of engineering. But the knowledge, the knowhow, was all in the heads of foreigners, many of whom could hardly speak English or spoke it with heavy accents.

As the public came to know more about the dangers of atomic energy, fierce local opposition arose in all quarters of the land to the construction of atomic-powered plants—finally a manifestation of a democratic response, although in most cases too late. Several such plants, although completed, are not operating owing to public opposition as expressed in legal actions. And some leading politicans have seen the wisdom of siding with public opposition, where there are apparently many votes to be found.

And as it finally turned out, at plants throughout the country where fissionable atomic materials were processed for the government weapons programs, there have been leakages down through the years of atomic radiation into the surrounding water and atmosphere, unknown to the neighboring residents. In some cases, local residents did not know lethal materials were being processed in their midst.

But in general, throughout the whole of atomic energy development and application, the public has been deceived or left in ignorance at every turn, leaving the credibility of officialdom very much in doubt.

Nor is it only with respect to atomic energy that there has been gross deceit by officialdom. Industrial hazards in general have been played down or denied all along for the benefit of private corporations. And here again it is a question of a trade-off. The trade-off is the item of greater costs to be avoided by more scrupulous vigilance and notification. And with greater costs the public itself will eventually prove balky. The public, in other words, wants complete safety but it is often unwilling to pay for it, an instance of simple irresolution.

The industrial hazards in question come from the labelling and handling of toxic materials, in some degree by the chemical and petroleum industries but also by other industries. Ordinary safety measures have been ignored as part of cost-cutting and the negligence of corporations has been ignored by officialdom. In this process, the broad public, the bedrock of ostensible democracy, has been repeatedly injured and corrective steps have been slow to take place.

One development among many illustrates what happened in the way of severely damaging the public interest. This was the case of the Johns-Manville Corporation, manufacturer of asbestos products. Asbestos was once applied in all forms of construction as freely as wood, steel, bricks or mortar. Yet insiders knew as long ago as the 1890s that it was dangerous if given frequent or continuous exposure. This was originally disclosed in England but records of Johns-Manville showed that company officials knew the dangers of asbestos dust, as recently as the 1930s.

In time, tens of thousands of workers in the asbestos industry were found to have a fatal and incurable disease and there was a reversal of attitude toward asbestos as its dangers were made known. Now asbestos was torn out of houses, office buildings and schools in a frantic attempt to get rid of the substance and Johns-Manville went into bankruptcy under the impact of law suits against it.

Why were not the dangers associated with this and other substances exposed in a timely fashion? It was the usual story of making a choice about where the public interest lay—in prompt notification or in continuing to treat the offending substance as harmless.

All along the government, under all administrations, has been extremely tender of the interests of corporations, feeling that they need to be protected for the sake of economic stability. The dangers to those exposed to the substances have been ignored.

It can, then, hardly be argued that the public, the core of what is referred to as popular sovereignty, has anything whatever to say in this as in many other matters. What happens in this and in all other instances of public hazards is that government does whatever it feels is most convenient to its own policy personnel, its elected officials. If it feels there is a lively possibility of retaliation by the voters at the polls for its non-feasance, it may act. But, on the other hand, even then it may not act as officials may be more closely allied with corporate offenders than with the government. For if they lose their government posts, they feel they will be provided for by their corporate friends. Unlike dictatorships that have no private economic sector, the United States is a country where there are plenty of roosting places outside the government for officials friendly to powerful private interests. One of the joys of privacy is that it may be affluent privacy.

The electoral democracy, then, has little to say about government unless it fully mobilizes itself to throw laggards out. And replacements who are expected to do better may be cut from the same bolt of cloth, so a mere change of administration does not produce improvement in the matters at issue. In any event, it takes a long time to mobilize a sufficiently large section of the public to influence public policy and even then the new policies may be heavily diluted by the opposition.

The general public in most instances is completely helpless because it is disorganized and very much at odds within itself— lacking knowledge, single-minded leadership and staying power. The national public must at all times also deal with many local and personal problems. It is, therefore, always easily defeated by determined entrenched interests.

XII

ALL EXPERTS on the subject of democracy stress that it is important that the voters know about the people and the issues they are voting for. Yet it can easily be shown that *all* the voters lack vital knowledge of their candidates, especially their presidential candidates. They also often lack such knowledge about candidates for Congress and for those seeking governorships and other local offices.

The public, for example, did not know that Woodrow Wilson was seriously ill, with alarming symptoms showing themselves as early as 1906. Moreover, his illness was of such a nature that it might affect his judgment, for it was neurological. Wilson's principal biographer, Arthur S. Link, says he was "either gravely ill or severely incapacitated at the time the country needed his leadership most." But Wilson's illness long antedated that time.

Anyone who wishes to read about Wilson's illness in great detail should consult the *Journal of American History* for September 1970 (Vol. 57, pp. 324-351). There one will find an article by Dr. Edward W. Weinstein, professor of neurology at the Mount Sinai School of Medicine of City University of New York. In this article, Dr. Weinstein points out that Wilson had a "long history of cerebral vascular disease" that produced "alterations in behavior and personality" during his presidential incumbency.

Dr. Weinstein traced Wilson's illness from 1896 when he had bouts of "nervous stomach" and "tension headaches" with high blood pressure. His condition was then diagnosed as cerebral vascular disease. The ensuing time up to Wilson's stroke in 1919 is referred to by Dr. Weinstein as the second phase of the disease. In this second phase, in 1906, Wilson, then President of Princeton University, woke up one day blind in his left eye, a fact never disclosed. A blood vessel had burst in his eye, indicating "a general disease of the arteries, probably high blood pressure." According to the doctor's account, Wilson's early adult life was marked by instances of depression, dyspepsia, colds, headaches, dizziness and feelings of dullness with a sense of numbness in his right hand, diagnosed at the time as neuritis, which although serious in itself was a mis-diagnosis.

The episode of 1906 was indicative of occlusive disease of the carotid artery, the major supplier of blood to the brain. In brief, Wilson's brainpower was affected by his congenital illness and Wilson after 1906 thought he might die at any moment.

Accompanying all these physical events were personality changes, producing in effect a different person. He was apparently in good condition when he entered the White House in March 1913, but in 1915, he had several days of "severe blinding headaches" and many so-called colds the exact nature of which were not disclosed.

In 1916, Wilson felt heightened tension, was extremely irritable and was intolerant of any opposition, displaying anger about trifling things.

At the Paris Peace Conference in April 1919, Wilson became ill after spells of irrationality with, as Dr. Weinstein reports, "high fever, cough, vomiting, diarrhea, and insomnia." His attending physician diagnosed his condition as "influenza." After his return home, Wilson, in October 1919, had a massive stroke, which was also concealed from the public. Although he was completely disabled, nobody knew of his condition and his orders were ostensibly transmitted through his wife, who was later accused of acting as President of the United States, secretly.

All of this was subject to a "cover up" for many years and the records of his attending neurologist, Dr. Francis S. Dercum of Philadelphia, were all destroyed after his death, in accordance with Dercum's will. This is a most unusual procedure with respect to medical records.

In the meantime, while in the grip of this serious mind-affecting disease, Wilson was making cataclysmic alterations in historical American foreign policy, with seriously disturbing long-term effects on the United States and western civilization. He dismissed Secretary of State William Jennings Bryan in 1915 for having advocated a course of traditional neutrality toward the warring European powers. Bryan had sponsored the nomination of Wilson and was responsible for many of the reform measures of Wilson's first term. Yet, for proposing strict neutrality in accordance with American tradition, he was sacked.

William Jennings Bryan was the real hero of this situation but as such he is unsung and has been made into a semi-comic figure by the media. The way this happened is that when cashiered by Wilson, Bryan had no place to go. Owing to his anti-corporate and pro-labor stands in the past, there was no place offered him in the private sector. So, in order to make a living, Bryan turned to lecturing, particularly to lecturing before Fundamentalist religious groups. In addition, he allied himself with the Prohibition movement, which led to his being dubbed "Grapejuice Bryan" for having suggested the use of grape juice instead of wine. He was also cartooned as "Bird's Nest Bryan" owing to his long, curled-up hair on the back of the neck, which was shown as the home of birds. Bryan, a true stateman, in personal deterioration, was made a figure of fun by the intelligentsia and his role in the Scopes "Monkey trial" in Tennessee in the 1920s intensified the ridicule to which he was exposed. But Bryan, as I say, was the real if unacknowledged hero of the war years.

By involving the United States in the war, Wilson doomed Britain and France to the very reduced circumstances they are in today. How this came about is as follows: All the European capitals of 1914-1916 were in charge of a nationalistic war party, which the tribalistic public in all countries enthusiastically supported. Germany thought she was so powerful that she could take on the world, which she did in the form of Britain, France, Italy, Russia and Japan.

The armies had become stalemated in trench warfare by the summer of 1916 and this seemed a propitious time in which a non-decision cease-fire might have been attained. But the war parties in Britain and France were especially opposed to any such cessation, even as the battlefield corpses continued to pile up. For, ever since the beginning of the war, they had been

encouraged to believe they could bring the United States into the
fray. Such encouragement had been constantly proferred by
Walter Hines Page, the U. S. Ambassador to the Court of St.
James's, who faithfully carried out the pro-British inclinations of
Woodrow Wilson.

But Wilson's pro-British attitude had quite opposite results for
Great Britain, illustrating Oscar Wilde's saying, "Every man
kills the thing he loves."

For Wilson's attitude encouraged the British government, and
the French government, to carry on the war to the limit,
spending its manpower without cessation. And with ultimate
victory, those governments were encouraged to force a punitive
peace on Germany, which was elected to pay for the war—a
politically popular but ridiculous notion. For, to pay the war
reparations imposed, Germany had to export manufactures at
whatever price it could get, disrupting markets for the "winners"
of the war. The idiocy of the Versailles Peace Treaty was pointed
out at once by the economist John Maynard Keynes, who was
present at the peace conference as an observer for the British
Foreign Office, in the book *The Economic Consequences of the Peace*
(1919). Everything destructive that was to occur during the next
15 years was, in general, foretold by Keynes.

That the Versailles Treaty was a huge mistake was shown by
its not being proposed again when Hitler was finally overcome in
1945. Then the terms of peace for Germany were lenient and she
was assisted back onto her feet with the United States Marshall
Plan. For it was now recognized that the Versailles Treaty had
spawned Hitler and Nazism in Germany. But by now the British
and French empires, which might have become frameworks for
large-area cooperation in the world, were gone, leaving in their
train crippled and warring members. Their disillusion was the
legacy of Wilson and the British and French governments of
1914-1919.

That Wilson's mind was affected by his illness is shown by his
Messianic flights of fancy in orations. The war, he said upon
America's entry into it, was being fought to "save the world for
democracy"—this in face of the fact that the czar of Russia and
the emperor of Japan, two absolute autocrats, were allies. The
war was also fought, he said, to end militarism in the world, with
the result that the United States is now the preeminent military

power of the world, its forces superior to *the combined armies of world history up to 1945!*

The Kaiser's proud army of 1914-18 was little more than a Boy Scout troop compared with American firepower and mobility today. Wilson's Fourteen Points were taken seriously by Germany, and helped in its sudden collapse, but they were superseded by the Treaty of Versailles, which the United States Senate refused to ratify.

Wilson's big idea, and one for which he is still revered by many "constructive" mentalities, was the League of Nations. This would be a body in which all the Powers would meet and arrive by rational measures at solutions to war-breeding problems. The United States Senate, for good reason, refused to allow America to join the League, which became a tool of its dominant members, Britain and France.

The League of Nations was succeeded after World War II by the United Nations, which in the main has been a world "talking shop" and nothing else. The United Nations, for example, can make no move without the assent of the five major powers on the Security Council. A veto by one member stops everything. The General Assembly, consisting of many countries with less power and authority than Hoboken, New Jersey, can do nothing except ventilate endless grievances, mainly against one or the other of the major powers. The United States—would you believe it?—is a frequent whipping boy of the Assembly, sometimes by virtually unanimous vote.

While conceding that it would be great if the United Nations were the framework for a rational world government, at the same time one should recognize, as Wilson and his followers did not, that the world does not really want any sort of rational government other than what each tiny entity would prescribe. We have here, obviously, a formula for conflict.

Wilson's League of Nations was only superficially a good idea. Intrinsically it was a very foolish idea, for mankind is not seeking a composition of its differences. It is seeking, in every entity, the installation of its own system of rule for everybody.

We come here to conceptions of mankind. From time immemorial, theologians and philosophers have projected a portrait of mankind as a highly superior and constructive creature. As Aristotle said, man is a rational animal, a statement that is not remotely true. Man is, on the contrary, the most dangerous animal on earth, dangerous to himself and to all other animals— so dangerous indeed that he is in need of formal government.

It is government alone that keeps individual men from destroying each other, contrary to the anarchists. But it is also the case that governments vis-a-vis governments defeat the whole purpose of government by engaging in warfare over relatively trivial differences, sometimes out of simple vanity. The basic proposition about mankind should be that it is a very dangerous animal and should be primarily approached as such. Man is not Mr. Nice Guy but is a Jekyll-Hyde creature, who must be carefully restricted. For at any moment he is apt to go berserk on an awesome scale.

In this connection, we should recall the allusion of David Hume (1711-1776), the great Scottish philosopher, to "the natural depravity of mankind" in his essay "That Politics May Be Reduced to a Science."

What is said here about Woodrow Wilson is said to bring out only one fact: the public does not know about significant factors affecting its highest officials, not only with respect to their health but their policies. Office-holders often have a secret agenda and part of Wilson's secret agenda was: help Britain.

In so resolving, he went straight against George Washington's doctrine of no entangling alliances. Wilson not only entangled the country in alliances but the United States today is tangled up in such a network of alliances that the government has no control at all of its destiny. The United States, through entangling treaties, can be involved in wars or other cataclysmic events without its volition. At any moment a large number of local despots have it in their power to force the United States into wars, without any declaration by Congress or order of the President. To a large degree, the United States is a giant puppet at the mercy of distant events over which it has no control.

The secret illness of Woodrow Wilson had this significance: it was a colossal personal achievement for Wilson to keep going in the face of such disability and to preside over a great government. This suggests great force of character, almost superhuman character. At the same time, a person able to carry on in the face of such personal adversity and anguish necessarily acquires an exaggerated sense of his own power. Hence, Wilson's assignment to himself of the Promethean role of reforming the world and banishing warfare from it.

Wilson's illness had, in evident fact, induced in him delusions of grandeur and he was using the United States as his special instrument. The pathological world we see today is the outcome of Wilson's feelings of moral superiority, justified on a personal basis but of tragic consequence when projected on the world. Other people, it is true, also had a hand in shaping that world.

In popular language, Wilson was as nutty as a Christmas fruit cake. And the fact was totally concealed from the electorate.

Wilson was by no means the last President whose physical and mental condition was kept as secret as possible from the voting public. Franklin Roosevelt was paralyzed from the hips down but many people were unaware of this until after he had been elected president four times, despite the fact that he was constantly photographed, even for moving pictures. The photographs, however, were all taken to conceal his condition. They always showed him either sitting down or standing up, on concealed braces. What the President's true condition was might have entered into the voting action of some citizens although whether it affected any of his decisions is not certain. As far as one can tell Roosevelt's decisions always had a rational basis.

Eisenhower's two illnesses while he was president were immediately known and they stimulated a call for physical examination and review of medical history of candidates for the office. Nothing formal has so far come out of this.

The next president, John Kennedy, it is now known had a serious illness called Addison's Disease. He was known to have this before entering the White House and his handlers were, during the election campaign of 1960, fearful that the fact might become known. Had it become known it might easily have given the victory to Richard Nixon for there was only a little more than 100,000 votes separating them in the election.

Lyndon Johnson was known to have had a heart attack before he ran for President in 1964, which only goes to show once again that the chief executive of the country may have personal problems of such magnitude that they affect his judgment. To every rational analyst, the involvement of United States forces in Vietnam by Kennedy and Johnson seems to be beyond explanation, intelligible only according to some unknown secret for-

mula. For it was not to combat communism that the United
States went into Vietnam, which was only a minor outpost of
communism. If not a secret formula at work the sending of
American troops to Vietnam may have been simple childish
rashness. And one does not like to think of an American
President acting childishly, flexing his muscles for simple
display.

But it is not merely the health of Presidents that is kept secret
from the voting public. It has come about that the entire "image"
of the President that is presented to the public is a gross
fabrication by a team of election specialists. These specialists
include speech writers (for few candidates write their own
speeches), authors, elocutionists, strategists who know what
words will affect different voting groups, make-up men, tailors,
hairdressers, stage designers from Hollywood, lighting experts
and many more arcane experts.

The task of all these people, composing the election team, is to
develop a fictitious character to take part in the election charade.
The election campaign is a charade because it has nothing to do
with the way the government will be run.

The object of the election campaign is to make the candidate
eligible to take the oath of office. This eligibility is acquired by
getting the most votes, so anything that generates votes is welcome.

Once the oath of office is taken, a winning candidate has a free
hand for the rest of his term. He is answerable to no one as long
as he stays within a reasonable expanse of constitutional territory, much of which is in fact in dispute. A winning candidate is
in possession of what the Romans called the *imperium*—that is,
command.

It is stressed for students in the schools that the President is
hedged about with checks and balances but history teaches us
that these can be circumvented. Furthermore, there are no
checks and balances at all bearing on the President with respect
to foreign operations. Here he has more power than ever did any
Roman emperor, and this is understood by most people. What
most people don't understand in the United States is that he has
peremptory power—no required discussion with anybody. The
President can, as Kennedy and Johnson showed, put the United
States into the most nonsensical, expensive and destructive war
one can imagine.

Most Americans don't know that the Constitution's framers were most disturbed about the presidential office, with many wishing to divide the presidency among a number of holders to check peremptory power. Many of these doubting constitutional delegates were persuaded to assent to the presidency as designed by the fact that George Washington would be the first occupant of the office. But not many Presidents have come near to Washington's performance in the office and it is doubtful even at this late date that Washington would assent to the overruling of his doctrine of "no entangling alliances" by Woodrow Wilson and Wilson's successors.

What most members of the public fail to realize, and this includes professors of political science among them, is that the government of the United States, once elected, has an absolutely free hand and is its own judge of its acts. Anyone who does not like what this government does has merely to wait until the next election when he will be allowed to vote against *a very small section of it*. Of 435 members of the House of Representatives, each citizen gets the chance to vote for only one, every two years. Of 100 members of the Senate each citizen gets the opportunity to vote for two within any six-year period. And a citizen may vote for a President, selecting usually one out of two major candidates, every four years. He never gets a chance to vote for a Federal judge. Furthermore, it is much the same in voting for state offices.

Most of the time even well-informed voters haven't any concrete notion of who they are voting for. The vote is a blind gamble, as proven on many occasions. For the voter knows no more about the lower candidates than he knows about the presidential candiates. *After* a term or two, a voter knows a great deal more about a presidential candidate. And after a single term the voters refused to reelect Hoover, Gerald Ford, Jimmy Carter and would surely have rejected Wilson had he been able to run for a third term. In the light of what became known about them after their incumbency it is doubtful if the voters would have reelected Warren G. Harding or John F. Kennedy. Voters in the American system are usually "flying blind" as far as knowledge about a candidate is concerned, especially about a presidential candidate. The reason for this is that relative unknowns are from time to time sprung on the public by the political parties.

It was the Constitution's framers idea that the Electoral College, meeting in detached assembly, would select for President one of the nation's "First Characters." This indeed was done up until about 1825, after which it became a free-for-all. About the only person in this century who was elected and might be describable as a "First Character" was Dwight D. Eisenhower. All the others were either unknown or relatively obscure or transitory persons. By means of the office, however, a person may become a "First Character," a case of the office exalting the man. Franklin Roosevelt was one such.

In this century, nearly every man who has stepped into the presidency has been a fictitious character as far as the electorate is concerned. All along, naturally, candidates for offices had concealed any negative factors in their background and highlighted all affirmative factors. However, in the newer refinements of this process, not only were all negative factors blotted out but the candidate was endowed with affirmative characteristics that he did not in fact possess. However, merely suppressing something like Wilson's serious illness amounted to presenting to the electorate a fictitious person.

As, to some extent, all candidates are wrapped about in a cloak of fiction one cannot in brief space review them all. For this reason I will show in only one case, that of John F. Kennedy, what was done. One could, however, do more or less of the same for all the candidates. Some successful candidates are seen by the public as more nearly themselves than others, as "naturals." Two such "naturals" were Truman and Eisenhower. Carter and Reagan, too, were pretty much of a "natural."

As to Kennedy, the person the public saw was a very serious and earnest young man, a highly patriotic combat veteran of World War II and a devout Catholic family man who had recently married a socialite. The press saw in Kennedy and his administration the elements of the Broadway musical *Camelot*, which was based on the legend of King Arthur's court. This was a gratuitous touch from outside the administration but was faithful, as the press saw it, to the ingredients it was presented with.

While some of the foregoing was true, such as Kennedy being a combat veteran and a nominal Catholic, most of it was false. The charming Kennedy the public came to know and with whom a large public fell in love was as fictitious as King Arthur.

The first problem Kennedy had to deal with was the conventional wisdom that no Catholic could attain the American presidency. People would not vote for a Catholic because most of them were Protestants, and many were Jews.

How this problem should be dealt with—ignored, soft-pedaled, denied or stressed?—was tested on a computer into which much demographic data was fed. The computer's answer was: stress the issue. And this was done. Kennedy ran as a devout Catholic who, however, would not be dictated to by the Church. His apparent Catholicism and religiosity was stressed even at his inauguration with Cardinal Cushing of Boston present in the brilliant raiment of his office for the administration of the presidential oath.

But Kennedy, although born into the Church, was no more a Catholic or otherwise religious in spirit than was Robert G. Ingersoll (1833-1899), whose soubriquet was "The Great Agnostic." It is doubtful that Kennedy was an agnostic, atheist or fideist, or had any universal outlook. What Kennedy was, intrinsically, was a secularist, a hedonist and a self-centered opportunist, and this showed in all his actions.

Not only did Kennedy blithely ignore the most urgent precepts of the Church but it is rare in history to see any self-designated prominent Catholic so conspicuously and repeatedly thumb his nose at those precepts. Before his marriage he ignored them with his very frank womanizing, about which many writers have taken note and which the Church stigmatizes as fornication. And after his marriage he also ignored church precepts with his continued womanizing, which the Church stigmatizes as adultery. Kennedy bedded, in the White House no less, a woman who was also a paramour of Sam Giancana, the Chicago ganglord.

There is, at any rate, a long trail of documented overnight assignations throughout Kennedy's adult life, suggesting that he was not only the most promiscuous but also the most compulsively priapic President the United States has ever had. None of this was known to the general public during his lifetime although various members of the press were well aware of his caperings.

Kennedy was no respecter of established authority at all,

constitutional or otherwise. This was shown immediately upon his entering the White House when he failed to consult his predecessor or anyone in the military about the feasibility of invading Cuba with an assembly of amateurs. Again, the account put out about the Bay of Pigs disaster was a tissue of lies. This story was that the invasion of Cuba by a hastily recruited group of Cubans and others was something that had been planned by the C.I.A. and that Kennedy upon entering the White House inherited this operation-in-being. According to the cover story, he let it go but at the last minute cancelled promised air support for it.

The fact, however, is (as carefully delineated by Professor Garry Wills in *The Kennedy Imprisonment*)[1] that there was no C.I.A. plan to invade Cuba. What existed was a guerrilla training operation that on Kennedy's order was accelerated into an invasion operation. The entire planning of the Bay of Pigs invasion was supervised by Kennedy himself, who chose the place of landing, the time and everything about the affair. When the hare-brained scheme failed, it was falsely said to be a legacy from the Eisenhower Administration. When asked about it, the former President said he had never heard of such an operation until it took place.

As Professor Wills says, "The truth is that Kennedy went ahead with the Cuban action, not to complete what he inherited from Eisenhower, but to mark his difference from Eisenhower. He would not process things through the military panels, let them penetrate Bissell's[2] secrecy. He would be bold where he accused Eisenhower of timidity. He would not send in the Army, Navy, and Air Force, but only Bissell's raiders. In all this he was the prisoner of his own rhetoric. As White House advisor Theodore Sorenson admits, his disapproval of the plan would be "a show of weakness inconsistent with his general stance."

All the while the man who had supervised the invasion of Hitler's Europe was only a phone call away. What the zero chances were for the Cuban operation Kennedy could have learned in five minutes, from the mouth of the master himself. But Kennedy felt he was more expert than any expert, despised

---

[1] 1981, pp. 232-54.
[2] The C.I.A. man in charge of the invasion force.

bureaucratic review. He also thoroughly under-valued Fidel Castro, who had successfully engineered a very thorough revolution and was adulated at the time by most of the Cuban population.

So little did Kennedy regard the opinion of others that he didn't hesitate to appoint as Attorney General his brother Robert, knowing that it would bring charges of nepotism.

Nor did Kennedy feel bound by the Consitution, resounding oath or not. And here he was little different from some other Presidents who have shown a strong tendency to wander outside the constitutional ball park even as a large public shouts hallelujahs to the great document of 1787. For John Kennedy and his brother Robert arranged to have known underworld figures attempt to assassinate Fidel Castro, who for unacccountable reasons had turned out to be a particular Kennedy object of hatred. In his election campaign, Kennedy had taunted the Republicans for having allowed a Communist regime to be established just 90 miles off U.S. shores. Yet Kennedy himself at the last minute had recoiled from allowing the air force to support the C.I.A. invasion.

While it is known the Kennedys were plotting Castro's assassination—contrary to the U. S. Constitution and the Ten Commandments—the American public even today does not realize the magnitude of the proposed operation. As Professor Wills says, "Operation Mongoose, the anti-Castro project, became the C.I.A.'s most urgent clandestine operation. Its base in Miami was the Agency's largest, with 600 case officers running 3,000 Cuban agents, 50 business fronts, and a fleet of planes and ships operating out of the 'fronts.' Lansdale was told to act quickly and he promised to bring Castro down within a year. Robert Kennedy did not want the man who humiliated his brother to gloat long over his triumph."[3]

What was taking place was a secret war being mounted against Castro, unknown to the American public. And lacking knowledge about all this, the American public naturally thought it gratuitous that the Cubans began installing Russian ballistic missiles, presumably with atomic armament.

This brought on the Cuban "missile crisis," for the handling

---

[3]*Ibid.*, 251-52.

of which the Kennedy forces are fulsomely praised—so skillful, so adroit, so constructive! Actually the "missile crisis" was the second of many disasters produced by the Kennedy Administration, the first being the Bay of Pigs operation. As Professor Wills points out, the placing of missiles in Cuba was a purely defensive act on Castro's part although not seen as such by the American public because of the secrecy of the attempts on the Cuban leader's life. With the Kennedys intent on getting his scalp, Castro, in defense, concurred in the missile emplacement to ward off these attacks—if worst came to worst.

Furthermore, the missiles in Cuba did not pose any grave or new threat to the United States or to American cities. It was Kennedy himself who had proclaimed the missiles "offensive and exaggerated their range," as Professor Wills points out. "It is understandable that he would not reveal all the American provocation that explained the presence of the missiles. But why did he have to *emphasize* the unprovoked character of their placement? He told the nation that the Russians had lied to him in promising not to send offensive weapons to Cuba. He said in his address on the crisis, 'The greatest danger of all would be to do nothing.' If he was chained to a necessity for acting, he forged the chains himself."

The actual hero of the Cuban missile crisis was Nikita Khruschev, who meekly ate dirt as Kennedy ordered the immediate withdrawal of the missiles, a grandstand play that brought him great applause at home. But Khruschev, who wanted to avoid war, paid for his deference to Kennedy by being dumped by the Politburo. He was replaced with a regime that was far more difficult for the United States to deal with. At the time of the crisis, many in the adminsitration expected that the Russians would at least attack American forces in Germany in retaliation for the gratuitous humilation at the hands of a sophomoric President. Kennedy gave Khruschev no room to "save face," but insisted on rubbing his face in the mud.

With the withdrawal of the missiles the American people were no safer than before but were still at great risk. For Russian submarines were prowling along the Atlantic coast at the time, with all major U. S. coastal cities in danger of being vaporized. And they still are today via Soviet ICBM missiles. Kennedy, in other words, relieved the American people of no threat whatever but conquered a crisis which he had himself conjured up out of thin air.

What is more, the atomic bomb, held to be a great American achievement, represents no protection for the United States or the American people. Before the creation of the bomb the U. S. was relatively safe either from foreign invasion or bombardment. With the invention of the bomb, duplicated quickly by the Russians and others, the U. S. instantly became as vulnerable to deadly assault as any primitive tribe. Had the Russians been less accommodating at the time of the Cuban missile crisis, the United States might have been in for some spectacular trouble.

As it was, Kennedy would involve the United States in deep trouble but the scene of action was to be Vietnam, a place few Americans knew anything about.

The idea of assassinating a neighboring dictator was nothing new in history but to pursue so vigorously such a minor figure as Castro suggests pathology, pure paranoia. At no time was Castro even a slight threat to the United States—an annoyance perhaps but no threat. And to arrange with the underworld, a constitutional enemy of the government, to have Castro killed was surely reckless, a pure stunt having no serious purpose other than a killing for killing's sake.

But sending 114,000 troops to Vietnam was even more reckless and ultimately more damaging than the pursuit of Castro. Nobody has been able to come up with an answer to the question of why troops were needed at all in Vietnam.

Eisenhower had refused to send them, despite suggestions that it be done, even though the U.S. had from the beginning been resistant to the Viet Cong of Ho Chi Minh, a wartime field ally of the United States against Japan. The U.S. had CIA operatives in Vietnam during Eisenhower's Administration, had in fact financed and supplied the abortive French attempt to re-take control of the country. The Vietnamese had fought the French to a standstill, with Chinese and Soviet help, thus showing they were not to be trifled with.

Even if the United States had been able to take the whole country with very little effort, the conquest would have represented a liability because Vietnam needed, more than anything else, a heavy infusion of fresh resources. As an economic proposition it wasn't worth a straw. What it seems to have been for Kennedy was another windmill to tilt against, another grandstand play reflecting delusions of grandeur. In order to anchor the project in some sort of reality there has been speculation that it may have been an operation to impress fellow Catholics, more especially New York's Cardinal Spellman, a friend of Kennedy's mother. Spellman, among other high Catholics, had been opposed to Kennedy's seeking the presidency in the fear that it might revive anti-Catholicism in the U.S. Nor was Spellman reassured by Kennedy's election victory.

Previously, in 1955, one of Spellman's wards had been placed at the head of the South Vietnamese government in Saigon. He was Ngo Dinh Diem, who for many years had been a refugee resident in the Maryknoll Seminary near Ossining, in the jurisdiction of Spellman's New York archdiocese. And Cardinal Spellman during the entire Vietnam War, as vicar-general to the U.S. forces, paid annual Christmas trips to Vietnam.

Something never made clear to the American public is that the Vietnam War was in part a religious war. The religion native to most Vietnamese is Buddhism; some adhere to Chinese-derived religions. But incidental to the French conquest of Indo-China in the 19th century, many Vietnamese were converted to Catholicism, and such were looked upon by the intensely nationalistic patriots as akin to traitors, collaborators with European exploiters. The South Vietnamese government in Saigon was established mainly by Catholics, many of them in flight from the Communists in the northern Hanoi region.

Whether any of this was the inspiration for Kennedy's late-budding interest in Vietnam is not known, but the Vietnamese had for centuries been extremely xenophobic and had fought continuously with invaders. So many elements were present that would argue to anyone who knew the scene that Vietnam was a tough nut to crack—xenophobia, native dislike of Europeans, religious hostility and the presence of a well-rooted Communist movement.

The United States was placed into Vietnam by Kennedy but as that adventure turned out to be disastrous in the extreme, Kennedy supporters have tried to distance him from the war by saying that he was on the point of pulling the troops out or planned to do so but was prevented by his untimely death and that it was Lyndon Johnson, his successor, who was responsible for the ensuing bloodbath. But this is manifestly false as Kennedy's brothers, especially Robert, were ardent supporters of the enlarging war in Vietnam, as late as 1967 when he seemed to be modifying his views.

Johnson, on the other hand, had been cool to sending troops into Vietnam, did not like the operation but was swung around in favor of it after Kennedy's death, probably by the Kennedy advisors whom he inherited.

Just as the blame for the Bay of Pigs was pushed over on to Eisenhower for allegedly having planned that ill-fated expedition, so blame for prosecuting the Vietnam war was heaped on Johnson. Kennedy himself, to hear his claque tell it, was blameless in all matters, the peerless king of Camelot.

Kennedy's curtailed administration, indeed, set the tone for the ensuing Johnson and Nixon Administrations. For it bequeathed to both of them its major problems, the Vietnam War and internal disruption that went with it. The semi-stability that had been achieved by the Eisenhower Administration after the long trauma of the Depression and World War II, all consequences of the Wilson policies of 1916-17, was shattered by the caperings of the Kennedy Administration.

Yet Johnson and Nixon are generally now seen for what they were while Kennedy remains for many a personally attractive and inspiring figure. Still, the media attempt to rekindle some of the fervor of the Kennedy days by commemorating the 25th anniversary of his assassination in 1988 seemed, somehow, to fall flat despite maximum attempts to bring back the heady days of the early 1960s. Too much was now too widely known about the intrigues of the Kennedys to justify looking upon the dead President as a martyr to freedom.

But history is not yet finished with the Kennedy story for the simple reason that the assassination and the reasons for it remain part of a huge unsolved mystery, a gigantic who-dunit. As long as this is unsolved it will continue to attract amateur sleuths. For, as careful analysis shows, the official Warren Commission Report holding that Kennedy was killed by a single marksman named Lee Harvey Oswald was as erroneous as anything whatever put out by the Kennedy Administration.

The currently ascendant theory about the shooting is that it involved at least two marksmen who were placed on the scene by gangland people with whom John and Robert Kennedy had had dealings in trying to assassinate Castro. The underworld is tied to the assassination because Jack Ruby, a product of the Chicago Capone gang, was the person who shot Oswald. Furthermore, it is known that in the underworld there were rumors that the President was to be "hit."

A mystery was how the Kennedys were able to press into their service so many unquestionably bright people. The way they rallied around John F. Kennedy one would suppose that the United States, in the tranquility of the latter Eisenhower years, needed emergency rescuing from malevolent forces that required herculean efforts. Was it that the scene seemed too quiet to people accustomed to decades of crisis? All these and many other questions are going to be explored by historians until every blemish discernible on the Kennedy era is brought to light. In any case, the Kennedy Administration rates, at this moment, as one of the big fiascos of American history.

The point of all this is that no matter how one may feel about the Kennedys, whether one sees them as demi-gods or as half-baked farceurs playing at statesmanship, the electorate neither knew about their orientation nor authorized any of their policies or activities. Nobody in the electorate called for the assassination of Castro, a special Kennedy project, nor for the infusion of conscript troops 8,000 miles away in Vietnam. Nor did the public ask for the establishment of the Green Berets as a counter-insurgency force, a pet project of President Kennedy in his consistent attempt, like Adolph Hitler before him, to by-pass the professional military establishment. Hitler always knew better than the General Staff; Kennedy always knew better than the Joint Chiefs.

The source of Kennedy's inspiration appears to have been the James Bond novels, which he helped make famous by his patronage. As for Kennedy's entourage of "the best and the brightest," the reason they were known to be such was that the country was simply told this as a fact. Just to be a member of the entourage was certification of omniscience.

I haven't related more than a few of the fictitious elements about Kennedy's public image. Like Wilson, he had a serious illness that his staff feared might become known during the election campaign of 1960: Addison's disease, a condition involving adrenal insufficiency that entails a wide spectrum of medical problems.

There is no doubt something of the "con man" about every politician but John F. Kennedy was without any doubt one of the most superb practitioners of the con man's art in American politics. Among the achievements for which he is given high credit is his initiation of the trip to the moon, which today rates as no more than an expensive technological stunt—dramatic, startling, but empty. As theater, down to the very end, the Kennedy Administration was outstanding. But it all added up to a painful and very expensive show, full of sound and fury, signifying disaster.

XIII

FROM THE LOWEST to the highest office, very little is known by the electorate about the candidates for any of the political parties, apart from what they are told by party publicists and ballyhoo agents. It is not only the presidency that is filled by fictional personalities. In olden days people had little true conception of their kings and the situation is much the same in the halcyon days of supposed democracy.

Furthermore, when any of the news media now begin to probe deeply into the background of a candidate for whom a considerable part of the electorate has conceived a fondness, there begins what is called a "backlash" against the offending news organization. For a part of the electorate does not like such probing against a favorite, does not want it to continue. In such a case, the electorate, instead of welcoming information, seems to be seeking ignorance. For in ignorance there may be bliss.

It is definitely not the case that the news media in the past have been especially enterprising in launching investigations into the backgrounds of candidates at any level of government. Prior to Watergate, the news media were usually in close collaboration with one candidate or the other. Partisan newspapers would directly and by implication heap high praise on one candidate and would blackguard another. Before the Watergate affair, most of the media on the national level, print and electronic, functioned pretty much as a public relations reserve for national candidates, especially for winners.

Watergate changed all that, at least temporarily. For one may expect the media to swing back to their old ways. What Watergate showed in stark documented terms was how different White House operations are from the way the media depicts them. The White House was found to be a humming beehive of conspiracies against a large variety of possible opposition groups, with illegal practices engaged in as a matter of course.

Many media people were chagrined to see how they had been roundly deceived, not only by the Nixon Administration but probably by earlier ones as well. There was, at any rate, a notably increased vigor in probing into the claims of candidates, many of whom had never scrupled about supplying an embellished or even fraudulent life history.

All of this was in sharp constrast to what went before, especially in the Kennedy Administration. In that period one saw what was perhaps the high-water mark of media sycophancy for a candidate, reaching its climax in the Camelot interlude. President Kennedy and his brother were presented as giant killers, especially after the way he had made Nikita Khruschev back down in the Cuban missile crisis. Played down in this picture was the fact that the crisis would never have arisen had Kennedy not withdrawn promised air cover from the Bay of Pigs invasion. Castro ruled in Cuba because Kennedy had failed to support what was later called Eisenhower's Bay of Pigs invasion.

On the other hand, during the Roosevelt Administration, 85 percent of the press was opposed to the New Deal and to the impresario who launched it. The fact that most of the public approved of Roosevelt was ignored.

More recently a backlash followed media questioning of E. Danforth Quayle's credentials to fill the office of Vice President. The inquiries of the press into his military and academic background were decried by Republican presidential candidate George Bush as a persecution of a highly qualified man.

Whether Dan Quayle could fill the presidential office if required still bothered many people. They can, however, be reassured because no President really runs the country alone, as popularly supposed. Each President is surrounded by party regulars as advisors, and these would almost certainly see that an insufficient man, provided he was tractable, did not do something idiotic. So there was really no cause to worry about Quayle taking over the *imperium*.

Gerald Ford, a political workaholic in the lower house of Congress for some 25 years, filled the office, being appointed by Richard Nixon, then threatened with impeachment, in the virtual certainty that Ford would pardon him. Ford was described by Lyndon Johnson as a man who couldn't walk and chew gum at the same time, and he more or less proved that Johnson had been right.

Running to succeed himself against Jimmy Carter, Ford, in television debate, vigorously denied that Poland was under the thumb of the Soviet Union. Anyone who had been a newspaper reader for the previous two decades knew that Poland was under a harsh tyranny propped up by Soviet bayonets. Every person of Polish descent in the United States knew this. Ford's lack of knowledge on this one point suggested enormous vistas of ignorance in his world outlook. That point alone may have cost him heavily in the election, although it was close both in the popular vote and in the Electoral College.

But as it seems, a large part of the electorate is not happy with negative information discovered about candidates who have, for some reason, captured the electorate's fancy and there follows a backlash of public opinion against perceived media bullying, as in the case of Dan Quayle. It would seem that a large part of the public is more interested in the electoral success of some individual than in having revealed his lack of qualification for a responsible office on which may depend the welfare and very life of millions of people. Is the candidate adequate to the job? This question seems lost in the flood of anger against the messenger bringing the bad news.

So, the public is initially misinformed about its candidates and a section of it resents seeing the cloak of misinformation penetrated. This section of the public quite evidently misunderstands the process in which they are participating as well as its objective. This section of the public also seems to confuse an election with a game in which the objective is to put a certain man over the goal line and declared a winner.

As to all those people who refuse to vote, and who are regularly lambasted for their non-performance, it seems at this point suitable to say a word. One should at first notice that they are entirely in harmony with the views of the writers of the Constitution, who did not want any popular voting for President, senators or judges. The public, in the view of the writers of the Constitution, was incompetent to judge about the personnel for these offices but was to be allowed to vote for the House of Representatives. The course of history, however, has led to voting for all offices except for Federal judges.

Elections are one thing and running the government is something altogether different. This being the case, nothing said, promised or implied in an election is binding on a candidate once he takes his oath of office. As soon as he takes the oath he is an actor in an altogether different system, in a republican constitutional system where his efforts are channeled and, in many ways, restricted.

The mere fact that someone has been *democratically* elected does not indicate that he is now part of a *democratic* government. In the United States, and mostly in western Europe, people may vote democratically but the government they get is something different: in Britain a constitutional monarchy, in France a republic. There is in fact, as I indicated earlier, nowhere on the face of the earth a recognized government that is indeed democratic. Democratically elected perhaps, yes; but itself in any way democratic, no.

There may, however, be degrees of democracy as between governments. Great Britain, for example, can be shown to be more democratic than the United States, even though such a proposition gives a painful wrench to many Americans who believe they live in a democratic paradise. The British government is more democratic because it must be more responsive to the public will than is the government of the United States at any time. The British chief executive officer, the Prime Minister, is responsive to a cabinet consisting usually almost exclusively of elected members of the House of Commons. The cabinet and the Prime Minister together are styled "The Government." But "The Government" must always win in the Commons on any vote that is also designated as a vote of confidence in "The Government."

Failure to win such a vote calls for a restructuring of "The Government" so as to win a vote of confidence or a general election to form a new House of Commons. If there is no such intervening vote "The Government" stays in office for five years, at which time there is automatically an election.

In other words, the directions of affairs in Britain can change drastically in a way that they cannot in the United States. For example, in the postwar years the Labor Party pursued a policy of nationalizing entire basic industries, on the theory that if the government ran them it would be in the interest of the common people. Failure of the industries to do well under government ownership led to a reversal or "privatizing" under Tory governments. Such wrenching back and forth of the status of industries as public and as private was, of course, unsettling and it could never happen under the United States Constitution.

For an industry to be nationalized in the United States, it would take more than a vote in Congress with the concurrence of the President. It would require an amendment to the Constitution, which is usually difficult to obtain owing to the necessity of having the concurrence of the legislatures, both houses, of three-fourths of the states. To obtain such a majority for such a proposal would seem to be virtually impossible.

The United States Constitution, then, is virtually frozen against anything like nationalization of an industry although if there were a widespread clamor for it, it could take place. But it would take more than a majority vote in Congress by some party that had recently won an election. The framers of the Constitution produced their document with the idea of preventing any sudden inspirational changes in the government. They wanted changes introduced only through a lengthy process that gave plenty of room for thought and discussion.

What the British nationalization and privatization movements suggest is that it isn't always well to be "more democratic."

Owing to their contextual uses, the words democrat and democracy are usually thought of as denoting something favorable. For would people vote for something to their disadvantage? It could easily happen that they would, simply by making a wrong or ill-informed choice, the same as any individual. Individuals constantly make decisions that turn out to be disadvantageous to them.

The words democrat and democracy usually signal something favorable, such as labeling some important person as very democratic. It might be supposed that an important person was aloof and withdrawn, conscious of his superiority, but to say he is very democratic is taken as a compliment. What is meant by this is that the person gives himself no airs, talks in a matter-of-fact and amiable fashion with all and sundry, high and low, and seeks no special privileges for himself. By transference or reference all uses of the word are taken to indicate something favorable. So, to say that someone was elected by a democratic vote, is to pronounce that candidate as a good choice. This is so even though it is known that a large number of rogues are regularly elected in the American political process, people who are later to be demonstrated in court proceedings as utter scoundrels. Not a few have been imprisoned and Richard Nixon narrowly missed prison.

A democratic election, then, does not guarantee a satisfactory official holding a certain office. The fact that democratic processes are in operation, in fact, indicates nothing, either favorable or unfavorable. It would seem to indicate that nothing secret is going on, but as we have seen there is a great deal of secrecy (from the public) and deception in candidates. Just because the process is open does not indicate that the public is fully informed about relevant matters.

It is often said that the United States is a democratic society, an assertion that should be taken with some great qualification. For the United States is full of institutions, all regulated according to law, that are nevertheless fixed in their operations, to be swayed neither one way nor the other by public favor or disfavor.

Consider hospitals. These operate according to predetermined principles designed by doctors and regulated by law. While laws concerning them may be changed from time to time, in general they operate according to a strict set of rules about which the public has little say, either directly or indirectly.

Consider next private schools, which were originally the only schools. Neither the subjects they teach nor their methods of teaching are subject to any government regulation or even suggestion. They may, like many so-called Bible colleges, teach the inerrancy of Biblical statements or they may, like the more acceptable schools, teach that Biblical statements are wholly mythic. And these that I refer to as more acceptable schools may teach the sciences, languages and philosophies in any manner of their own choosing, without government direction.

Most schools today are government-operated, so-called public schools, from elementary schools to universities, but these differ little in their curricula from the private schools except that in their lower grades they tend to present an idealized picture of the government itself.

Local public opinion in the United States is allowed to determine the curricula of the lower schools and the high schools but this is seen increasingly as detrimental to a sound education. Following democratic cues, many public schools—according to professional critics—have strayed from the path of sound education to a policy of catering to local whims.

Private schools, in any event, are free of governmental dictation and regulation.

Although established under the Constitution and the laws and regulated in some particulars by special laws, corporations operate without the least governmental or democratic direction. Approval or disapproval of a corporation comes through public patronage of its products and services. Apart from this, and the application of extant laws, corporations are fixed independent bodies in society, allowed to function pretty much as they please over a wide range of possibilities.

The general institutional structure of society, then, while not absolutely rigid, is relatively very much so against any democratic clamors coming from the surrounding society. While all parts of it may be altered, any change must be very gradual and any fundamental change must be carefully considered in elaborate processes.

Democratic restlessness shows itself against this institutional structure very much as does a restless sea against a granitic breakwater, constantly denied sovereignty. The government, far from being a passive tool of the people, is definitely their regulator. It can be altered, or made to alter course, but only very gradually, piecemeal.

What, then, is there to democracy? Is it a total illusion? Not at all. Democracy itself is something very fragmented, necessarily so as it is composed of the opinions of many.

Where we find democracy is, always, outside of government. Within government most matters are fixed, bound up in arcane laws.

Democracy involves the free creative powers of people, for good or ill. One sees constructive democracy at work, for example, in voluntary associations devoted to the achievement of some objective. A perfect example of democracy is the organization Alcoholics Anonymous, formed many years ago by two men to assist others in overcoming addiction to alcohol. All such self-financed self-help organizations, many modeled on Alcoholics Anonymous, are examples of democracy.

Again, organizations formed to advance certain causes through the wide participation of many people are surely manifestations of democracy. These petition and sometimes influence government.

Not only does the Constitution, as originally formed, permit democratic behavior on the part of people but in many respects it positively requires it. Many of the provisions of the first ten amendments to the Constitution so enjoin a more or less democratic behavior on the populace. And such provisions are, from time to time, resisted by large numbers of the populace itself, which in such instances shows no desire to be at all democratic. It is a mistake to assume that any large part of the populace wishes to submit itself to democratic rule. Most of the populace simply wants its own way, like any dictator.

The First Amendment forbids the denial or official establishment of any religion, expresses tolerance for a multiplicity of religions or for no religion. It is regularly opposed by all who wish to make their own religion exclusive or to bar irreligion. It expresses both freedom for any religion and freedom from any religion, making the matter of religion purely optional for everybody.

Further, it guarantees freedom of speech and of the press, without which one could not take the least step toward democracy. Yet both of these freedoms are often opposed by elements in all layers of the populace from time to time, suggesting the populace itself is not wholly democratic. Also guaranteed are the freedom of assembly and petition, and we often see these freedoms exercised by marching and demonstrating groups which, indeed, are often protesting against the exercise of some lawful freedom by others.

Most of the other amendments to the Constitution provide guarantees against the gross abuse of people by government officials and, in fact, make freedoms possible. They insure what is called civil rights.

It should be noticed, however, that under the United States Constitution, most violations of civil rights are perpetrated not by officialdom, but by citizens vis-a-vis other citizens. Such violations constitute what is known as crime, involving the forced or surreptitious deprivation of life, health, tranquility, liberty and property of law-abiding citizens. The United States has the greatest volume and rate of crime of any industrial nation, owing in large part to a polyglot, uprooted, unstable population. Most violations of civil liberties come not from government (contrary to claims of civil liberties organizations) but from individual civilians.

The statistics, taken from the *U. S. Statistical Abstract* for 1988, tell the story. In 1986, there were 19,527 murders reported by the police, 59.1 percent from guns. For the same year, there were 543,000 robberies, 3.24 million burglaries and 7.25 million larceny-thefts and 1.2 million motor vehicles stolen. All of these are the reported crimes; many others are simply unreported. The number of cases of forcible rape for 1986 was 72,626, with 17,504 attempted rapes reported. Much rape, however, authorities say is not reported.

Persons arrested in 1986 totalled 10.39 million, a phenomenal number. In the same year there were 87,585 cases of arson. No less than one quarter of all the households in the United States were directly touched by crime in 1986, reflecting a fearful guerrilla assault on society.

At the same time, prisons and other centers of detention were filled to 115 percent of capacity! More prisons were needed as governmental budgets were all strained as a result of wastage of money, notably some $200 billion in the undeclared Kennedy-Johnson Vietnam War.

As of 1985, an aggregate of 2,905,700 people were in what is described as "correctional detention"—255,000 in jails, 503,300 in state and Federal prisons, 277,400 on parole and 1,870,100 on probation.

The total cost of the criminal justice system in 1985 was $45.6 billion. Yet the average time served in prison by the inmates was surprisingly low in relation to the length of sentences. In 1986, prisoners released for the first time were sentenced on average to serve 34 months but were released after 15.6 months. Those paroled were released after 26.7 months on sentences averaging 76.6 months. Those who served full time served an average of 11.4 months of 18 months sentenced.

Certain crimes drew longer periods of incarceration. For example, 29 kidnappers sentenced to serve 251.6 months (20.9 years) served 85.7 months (7.1 years) when first released. And 886 robbers were first released after serving 46.5 months on the average out of an average sentence of 128.5 months. Most sentences in terms of time served, however, are relatively light and the pattern prevails extending backward past 1970.

Sentences served are very lenient, almost always, in the light of media reports at the time of trial. Then it is common for the media to report that a defendant, if convicted of 38 counts, faces a possible prison term of 175 years, or something equally ridiculous. It is often a let-down for the attentive reader when the person is convicted and then sentenced to a year of probation or six months' imprisonment.

When one goes on to consider the great amount of injury caused by reckless behavior in the populace, it is clear that the democracy—that is, the elements outside government—are far from orderly. And although public opinion favors longer sentences it does not provision the government with enough money to house culprits. The questionable amount of order in society outside of government—leaving aside the question of order in the government itself—should throw into some relief the claim that this body of people is capable of regulating itself.

A more interesting aspect of American society is thrown into relief by the crime statistics. It is the general claim that American citizens enjoy more personal liberty than those of any other country that ever existed, and this claim appears to be true. What is overlooked in trumpeting this claim, as politicians commonly do, is that many of these free citizens are free to prey on other citizens, and freely do so. To guard their civil liberties, then, American citizens must keep watch on two fronts: vis-a-vis the government and vis-a-vis everyone around them. For with 25 percent of households directly touched by crime of some sort in one year the assault on the citizenry is quite general.

It is often stressed by observers how roughly the Soviet government treats its citizens, how they are herded into labor camps and pushed about by the K. G. B. The Soviet so treats its citizens—or did until Mikhail Gorbachev took charge—because they had violated one or the other of stringent rules laid down by the government. Among these rules was that one may not decry whatever it is the government does.

Now, in order to avoid rough treatment by the Soviet government, all that was necessary was for Soviet citizens to observe all the rules, most of which were very restrictive and onerous, making life very much like being in a general prison without bars per se. If one observed all the rules, one was not, in general, molested.

But in the United States, one may be observing all the rules and yet be in quite constant danger of losing one's life, endangering one's health or being crippled or otherwise damaged for life, as thousands of people are every year. For doing nothing forbidden, a goodly percentage of Americans get far worse treatment than Soviet citizens who deliberately try to thwart the government. This may be taken as a footnote to American liberty.

The reason American public opinion, at least until now, has come to favor the predator rather than the victim of crime is that it has had a more immediate view of the predator. This person has been caught and he seems like a helpless animal in a trap, surrounded by heavily armed officers. As he goes on trial the full weight of government is seen arrayed against him, including the evidence, so that he is now distinctly an underdog, a favorite of sentimentalists. The crime victims, on the other hand, are out of sight, their sufferings less vivid.

It is easier to collect money from sentimentalists for the trapped criminal, civil rights organizations have found, than for the victims of crime. There are no organizations to serve victims but there are many well-financed organizations to defend criminals in the trap, all the way up to the electric chair. The victims are largely a blur in the background, of little concern to vote-seeking politicians who solicit the support of civil rights organizations.

What we see here, in a knotty situation, is the world turned topsy-turvy, on its head, where upside-down signifies rightside-up.

As to the death penalty, it has virtually disappeared in the face of nearly 20,000 willful, free-lance homicides per year. At the end of 1986 there were 1,519 persons under sentence of execution but in the year only 18 were executed, 16 of these in southern states. Opponents of the death penalty say it does not deter absolutely and for this reason should be abolished. But no punishment for crime whatever deters absolutely, as history shows, because some persons are reckless and others imbued with a gambling spirit. And while the death penalty is less and less used, the total of willful homicides steadily rises.

In summary, the general democracy is not particularly law-abiding as a whole although it is spottily so and is constantly ravaged within by its own lawless members, who seem to inspire more sympathetic concern than do the victims of crime.

Not only is there this great volume of crime taking place, year by year in an ascending curve, but social agencies report that six million American children are routinely neglected or abused. According to the *Statistical Abstract*, in 1985 there were 1,928,000 cases of maltreatment of children, including deprivation of necessities, minor and major physical injury, sexual and emotional abuse, and various other injurious actions. For 1984 (the latest year available), 69.9 percent of these children were white, 19.1 percent were black, 9.3 were Hispanic and 1.9 were of some other group. Nearly half of these children came from homes receiving public assistance and 37.4 percent from homes headed by a single female.

The *Abstract* does not give data for the children who are simply neglected and are subject to report by private social agencies.

At the same time, while all these children are being maltreated or neglected, crowds of demented or at least misguided citizens are staging violent protests against the laws that permit abortions which at least have the aim of reducing the number of unwanted pain-wracked children in the world. Contending that they stand for "the right to life" for every fertilized human egg, the protesters nevertheless seem wholly disinterested in the bundles of pain represented by six million neglected and maltreated children.

In the meantime, American society prides itself on its concern for its children, the apple of the hypocritical eye. And politicians, like carrion vultures, see the opportunity for picking up votes among the abortion disputants. Some of the politicians work both sides of the street.

XIV

BUT THE IDEA of "indirect democracy," put forward by Professor Sidney Hook as noted earlier, will not down, as it seems, somehow, plausible. The theory of an indirect democracy takes its form owing to the view that elected officials are delegates of the voters. The United States Constitution, however, nowhere suggests that this is so.

People often say "their" congressman or senator is "their" representative. But, constitutionally, these officials are representatives of a congressional district or of a state, not of the members of that state or district, individually or collectively. A lawyer or a doctor or a specified agent can, indeed, represent a person in his individual capacity. But neither a lawyer nor a doctor nor an agent could possibly represent a multitude with conflicting interests and demands. Somebody in that multitude is bound to be unrepresented and as a matter of fact all are bound to be unrepresented some of the time or even all of the time.

Neither a congressman nor a senator, nor, for that matter, a President, is the delegate of the electorate but rather the representative of a jurisdiction—a congressional district, a state or the country as a whole. None of these elected officials is under any obligation, constitutional or othewise, to do the bidding of any portion of the electorate.

The Constitution is very precise on this point. Article VI at the very end of the Constitution states that all Federal and state legislators and all executive and judicial officers "shall be bound by oath or affirmation to support this Constitution." No oath is taken to be guided by public acclaim or outcry.

We know this oath is in some cases violated, as when an officeholder is convicted of crimes. For the year 1986, there were convicted 523 Federal officials, 71 state officials and 297 local officials. These convictions took place in Federal courts (*Statistical Abstract 1988*).

The oath may also be violated in other instances that are not brought to adjudication.

But the numerous instances in which serious injury is brought by government action against members of the populace show that any idea of an indirect democracy at work, seeking to advance the individual interests of the citizens, is completely out of the question.

Where can we show such serious injury? It can be shown both easily and plainly in the reckless operation of plants for processing nuclear materials that are scattered about the country and under the jurisdiction of the Department of Energy. Investigations the results of which were announced in 1988 showed that as many as 30 nuclear processing plants in the surrounding region were repeatedly releasing—via air, water and land—radioactive emissions harmful to the health of residents, especially those living downwind. In such regions, abnormal rates of cancer in children and adults have been found. (See *The New York Times*, October 26, 1988, p. 1, and earlier accounts in the same period.)

The known dangers also of asbestos, kept from the public with government collusion, provide a similar example of official indifference to the health of workers, many of whom were engaged in government projects such as the building of ships in wartime.

It is the duty of the government, constitutionally, to see to the welfare of the people, and not to warn them of known dangers is hardly to show much concern. Now, it is not being argued here that the government was totally indifferent to public health. What is being argued is that the government was not *democratically* concerned. The government, as part of a republic, was *institutionally* concerned and made a decision on behalf of the total institution, for the apparent benefit of the total institution.

As it is expressed in popular terms, there was a trade-off, involving a great deal of presumed good in return for a certain amount of evil. One sees such a trade-off in war when a commander orders a certain body of troops to make a rearguard stand, thus being sacrificed, in order to allow a larger part of his command to escape. Although he may not despise the men in the rearguard, may in fact prize them most highly, the commander is not the delegate of the troops, bound to protect them at all costs.

However, the protests of the public on learning of its exposure to hidden dangers for "reasons of state," demonstrate that this is not the way it feels, but that it should be protected at all times by "its" government. For the public feels it is in a democracy where everybody is or should be treated equally by the government. As events show, however, this is not so and the public is simply mistaken in its belief.

That a democracy is not in operation can be illustrated in many other ways.

There are, for example, the vast amounts of money spent to elect candidates at all levels. Neither the general public nor the public treasury pays these election expenses except for matching funds given to presidential candidates. For the latter, private contributions under certain limits are matched with public funds.

But all other elected officials must finance elaborate and expensive election campaigns, involving armies of paid campaign workers, and such financing runs into millions of dollars. In *The Best Congress Money Can Buy* (1988), Philip Stern presents the data showing how Senators in the course of their six-year term stock fantastically large campaign warchests running into many millions of dollars—in fact, with no top limit at all.

Money financing elections has a long history, going far back into the 19th century right after the Civil War. One thing it certainly shows is that the multitude is not in control of the political process, that "one man, one vote" has little meaning when push comes to shove.

The money now funding elections is collected by what are called Political Action Committees (PACs), which are permitted by law. There are hundreds of these established mainly along economic lines by industries but also others to fit professional and labor perspectives. These committees allocate funds. All the participants deny, however, that the purpose of the funds is to influence government decisions and legislation, and anyone who accepts this denial as valid for one second should, in my opinion, have himself certified as mentally retarded. Everyone is a thorough-going boob who believes this for an instant.

Here is how it works. The PACs giving the money say it is simply to allow them "access" to the recipient, to gain his ear from time to time. And it is true that the PACs of political donors in general do not attempt to dictate a whole schedule of activities for the recipients. But whenever the PAC givers feel threatened or disadvantaged by any ruling or piece of legislation they make use of their "access." They then paint such a dire picture of what is sure to happen to them, and possibly also to the country, that the recipient has materials for several nightmares and sleepless nights.

It may happen, too, that the recipient is torn by some other commitment he has made so that, even though feeling sympathetic, he must turn down the PAC representative. He may, however, temper his turndown in many ways, saying he must go in a different direction, but that if the situation gets too bad for the PAC, he may switch and delay matters, etc.

Also, there may be a conflict among PACs, causing an official or legislator to choose, which is difficult but sometimes necessary. PACs, and political contributors, do not always get their way but much of the time they surely do, and they definitely come out ahead of disorganized clamors from the general population. Organization always triumphs over disorganization. Revolting slaves were always beaten down by the Roman centurians.

And although there may be rivalry among the PACs, the net effect of the entire structure is pretty much to preserve the *status quo* against demands from the general populace for one change or another. There is, however, always change but—and here is the fact—it is always less than what was asked for. The general populace, at least the most disaffected part, usually gets far less than it requests. As the French say, everything changes, yet everything remains the same. Ideal goals are never attained.

The set of officials in place, more or less secure with PAC support, is favorably disposed toward the general public, with the proviso that nothing will be done to unduly disturb the PAC contributors. This means fundamental changes demanded by the disaffected will definitely not be made. The marchers and protesters will just as definitely not overcome.

As indicated earlier, elected officials are not delegates of the voters in any sense, either the voters as individuals or collectively. They are, however, more nearly the delegates of PACs or of those who individually put up the money for their election. Once a man is elected he may secretly favor anyone he chooses to favor.

Organizations committed to the support of democracy, such as Common Cause, for example, are furiously opposed to the PACs and regularly fulminate against them in print and via the airwaves. Similarly, organizations and individuals for decades have decried the vast amount of money amassed to win elections, but without reducing such expenditures—which, in fact, have grown steadily. It would seem that the power of crucial political decision rests with those having the most money. In any event, they cannot be ignored.

There are thousands of areas in which the PACs and political campaign donors of any kind control the situation. Take the question of environmental sanitation. A very large and voluble public is opposed to the dumping of wastes, especially toxic wastes, in any part of the environment. So strong has the movement become that it has succeeded in having Congress pass tough laws and establish an Environmental Protection Administration. Environmental cleanliness is highly popular.

In the meantime, hundreds of locations have been discovered that are severely polluted with toxic wastes, a danger to people living nearby, with water, soil and even air affected.

Yet, despite the public clamor, progress toward cleaning up these toxic sites has been both slow and expensive. Instead of being forthrightly sorted out and cleaned up, the way ships and airplanes were built in wartime, there seem to be invisible barriers delaying the process. What about democracy? What about the voice of the people?

The delay is induced by officialdom, which listens to people who have access. These are campaign donors and consist of the representatives of chemical companies, oil companies, manufacturers of a wide variety of products and the like. These companies have for more than 100 years simply disposed of dangerous waste products by dumping them into the nearest drainage system and nearby empty land, there to seep into the water table below and eventually to poison drinking water. The environmentalists want the companies to stop such dumping and dispose of the wastes in some safer manner. This can be done but at tremendous additional cost, which must be added to the price of products to the disadvantage of consumers.

Nevertheless, the screws can be put on so tightly that industrial companies must comply, at whatever costs. They do, however, have a recourse, and that is to transfer operations abroad where there would not be such serious objections to their waste products. Many underdeveloped countries would welcome these companies. In this fashion many industries, feeling overwhelmed by the demands of organized labor, simply have moved operations abroad, thereby costing jobs for thousands of Americans.

Labor proved it could get higher wages. And management then proved it could move abroad or robotize operations as in the auto industry. The same thing can happen if companies are pressed too hard on waste disposal.

As to waste disposal in general, it is one of the looming, expensive problems in the future of industrialism. With a constantly increasing population, aided by much legal and illegal immigration, this problem is going to become gigantic for the United States.

Something the environmentalists overlook is that they themselves are a major part of the problem. Every person who drives an automobile, or who uses a bus or taxi, is a polluter, both direct and indirect. All such users support the industries that produce the instruments of pollution. It can often be shown, as a matter of fact, that the most vehement public protesters are agents for the condition against which they are protesting, which shows the basic incoherence of democracy, a fact recognized by the framers of the United States Constitution.

What the environmentalists are protesting against, really, is industrialism. The conditions they seek can be found only by going back prior to the Industrial Revolution. There is no safe place for industrial wastes except possibly distant deserts and the element of cost would be a factor in transporting the wastes there. At the same time there are environmentalists and ecologists who see great value in the deserts of the earth.

But it can be shown even more decisively that the rank and file has no control over events, either directly or through delegates. One shows this simply by the citation of a staggering bit of statistical data.

The American Institute for Economic Research reports in its *Economic Education Bulletin* for August 1988 that the politicians and money managers "have embezzled by the inflating process the surplus product of all who produce. Few fully understand the success of this process. In just four and one-half decades, our planners have taken $6,300,000,000,000 (trillion) from the savings of the Nation's 'forgotten citizens,' those who mistakenly relied upon the dollar and dollar-denominated assets for a store of value."

As most of the public finds economic terms opaque, a word of explanation may be in order: "The surplus product of all who produce" means the savings of people who work. Such savings were in the form of bank accounts, bonds, life insurance policies, mortgages and long-term government securities like so-called U.S. savings bonds.

Through inflation the value of all these savings was quietly removed so that when they were put to use in the purchase of goods and services they bought much less. The face value of the savings remained the same, but the purchasing power declined sharply.

Inflation is generally spoken of as though it were a natural phenomenon, like a spell of bad weather. But inflation is man-made, by governments. It is manufactured, to order. It is simply brought about by printing money to pay for expenditures going beyond tax collections. Tax collection increasingly incenses large numbers of citizens, who see their disposable income thus snatched away. They therefore resist taxation.

But governments, interested in catering to other elements of the population with supportive programs (and also carrying on its routine duties of defense in a dangerous world), simply launch these programs and pay for them with newly printed money. Having many large printing presses and an endless amount of paper, the government can easily drown the world with money.

But so much money, readily available, drives down the value. What makes money valuable is its relative scarcity. Unscarce money becomes worthless money, mere paper.

As money depreciates in value, workers must necessarily be paid more of it to sustain at least a minimal standard of living in the face of rising prices. Any of it held in reserve, in savings for a rainy day, steadily depreciates. Money in the bank becomes like the cake of ice people used to have delivered every few days before the era of mechanical refrigeration. A man brought the ice, which was put into the ice chamber of an icebox. But after a few days it was gone. Where had it gone? Nothing had been lost because it had simply melted, and the water had flowed into a drip pan underneath. All that had been lost was the *power* of the ice. One now needed a new cake of ice to maintain cool temperatures for food.

In the same way, nothing has been lost in bank deposits, which the government insures. The funds have merely turned into water, their original power gone. The dollar of 1940 has lost more than 90 percent of its purchasing power. A package of cigarettes costing 15 cents in 1940 now sells for $1.70. This sum would have purchased eleven packages in 1940. Any money left in a bank account since 1940 has suffered proportionately.

During this process, people who put their savings into first-class real estate or established stocks fared much better because such investments tended to preserve their relative values, moving in market price counter to the trend of inflation. A man or group of men, for example, who owned a central city hotel prior to World War II in which rooms rented for $5 per night, a fairly standard rate, might still own such a hotel but now the rooms would rent for $75 to $100 per night. All operating costs would be greater than before but so would the net operating income, which might have the same purchasing power as the prewar income. The capital value of the investment has been retained, despite inflation. And so with real estate in other than deteriorating neighborhoods.

People who invested in established stocks also fared better—and here one should emphasize the word "established." For there are thousands of stocks around whose value is highly problematical and even established stocks may at times be overpriced, so that one can lose money buying them.

But in illustration of what I mean, let me tell a personal story. In 1950, my mother, a lifetime working woman, came to me for advice in handling her savings upon which, in addition to a modest Social Security payment, she depended. Her savings were in three percent U. S. government savings bonds, and I advised their immediate sale. She was reluctant to sell them, as in her opinion the United States government was the finest thing that God had ever created. In response to my insistence, and probably because her native self-reliance was failing, she gave in, sold the bonds, and bought a handful of public utility stocks I recommended as a safe investment.

What happened was that her income from her savings was at once more than doubled, and over the next 20 years until her death, her stocks quadrupled in market value while the income steadily increased. She left her small estate to her grandchildren. Now, had she not made this investment switch, at her death her savings would have retained their original stated value but would be greatly depreciated in purchasing power. And her income all along from savings would have been far less, and of diminishing power.

Now, hearing stories like this, and being convinced by them, the average citizen may rush out and buy some real estate or stocks—a prime mistake. For all investments should be approached skeptically, with a view to discerning flaws in claims for them.

Right now, in early 1989, the general prices of stocks and real estate seem to me to be too high. In this I may be wrong and the future alone will determine. But if there should be a decline of prices in what remains a cyclical economy it seems to me that well-managed, no-load mutual stock funds are a better repository for savings than an "insured" bank account. What is insured in such an account is the dollar amount, not the purchasing power.

Many people, however, despite the bad track record of the government, depend upon it to do "the right thing." The government itself will survive; of that we may be sure. But in the interval there will be many citizen casualties, as in an advancing victorious army. So, if you are a government person, be of good cheer.

It seems necessary to me to stress the full significance of what has been said. There is much public congratulation over the fact that inflation has been reduced from ten percent annually to around four percent. But a steady rate of inflation at only two percent will, in 15 years, halve the value of any savings account. In general, savings for a rainy day are accumulated by people who work and who, the politicians claim, are the salt of the earth. Yet the material interests of these folk, whom one would figure to be the pets of any democracy, are flagrantly undermined. It seems to me to be a case of the governmental sheep dogs slowly devouring the sheep, which could not happen if democratic conditions prevailed.

Until recently in history, most people turned for surcease from their ills to God, to whom prayers were regularly directed. With the growth of secularism, however, many people have lost faith in the existence of God but have acquired strong faith in government, which has become something of a divine being to many people. But government cannot deliver all that many people crave for the simple reason that it does not have the resources, and not even the biggest governments such as the United States or the Soviet Union have such resources.

The wherewithal for the betterment of mankind can only come from the talents and labor of individual citizens, operating in a system of order guaranteed by government. And what such talents and labor can produce has a finite limit far short of the demands of a multitude. There is not enough money, gold and precious jewels in the entire world, for example, to meet all the popular demands of record in the United States alone.

The demands go far beyond the resources, as has been shown by the collapse of socialism in the Soviet Union. One thing the Soviet reversal shows us once again is: you cannot lift yourself by your bootstraps. The same rule applies to the United States.

It is an ironic fact that much of the impetus for the construction of the United States Constitution came from an abhorrence of inflation, at that time centered in the state governments with their proclivity to issue paper money, unbacked by any specific resource. It is one of the triumphs of elective democracy, however, that the printing-press-money crowd has conquered the constitutional government.

Leaving the rights or wrongs of the situation aside, as we are not here concerned with those, it should nevertheless be plain that the government has let down a body of millions of hardworking savers by not only failing to preserve the value of their savings, but deliberately undermining it.

Certainly this cannot be construed as a democratic act, and it is not a democratic act. It is, however, a republican act, by an independent governing entity known generally as the State or, in Latin, *res publica*. What it shows is that the public, and more especially the prudent and steadily working part of the public, has no control over the acts of government. The public may have some say about the top personnel of the government, about who takes charge, and it may have some say about those that are retained at stipulated election intervals. But beyond this it is entirely at the mercy of the calculations and manipulations of the governing professionals, the politicians. Against these, each individual citizen has only his own wit, understanding and knowledge, which in most instances don't amount to enough.

The public generally is a pushover for the politicans, easily swayed in a variety of directions.

In summary, government and people mutually influence each other but government wields more and weightier influence. While the government may be democratically elected, the fact of its democratic election does not make it democratic.

The framers of the Constitution, in allowing members of the House of Representatives to be elected by the citizenry (not all even of the white males of the time had suffrage) recognized what they called "the democratic principle." The "principle" here referred to was popular voting for government people. The framers did not think that this made for a democratic *government*, and with the recognition of this same principle in the selection of the President and senators, it did not make the government itself any more democratic than when it was originally founded.

It is argued by supporters of the democratic idea that the ability of the public to select its candidates and install them in office makes the process democratic. Unfortunately, the public has no role at all in the selection of candidates in the sense that one selects goods in a department store or supermarket. Selection for an election boils down to choosing among a restricted number of virtually unknown candidates and guessing which one is the best for the country. In the process, a few turn out to be amazingly good while many emerge as abominable—a game of chance.

How would it be possible to get better candidates? It would be relatively easy if enough people really cared, which they evidently do not. One would simply train them from youth onward, the way army officers are trained in most countries and judges are trained in France. Schools with special programs would train people eligible to stand for public office and would keep close track of their lifetime careers. Judges would be similarly trained.

Excluded from all elective officeholding would be everyone who had not undergone the requisite training and supervision, especially the latter. More could be said along these lines but enough has been said to suggest that all has not been done that could be done to obtain the best governors.

The public would now be able to select its candidates from among people certified as qualified and with a fully open career track record.

As matters now stand, plausible but basically unqualified adventurers are free to seek and attain any and all elective offices in the system with the acts of many of these political adventurers demonstrably inimical to the best interests of the common man. For my part I find it more comforting to be in the service of a competent trained general than to serve under a careless amateur butcher.

XV

FROM TIME IMMEMORIAL, the politician has had the reputation of being a dissembler, one who disguised his objectives so as to frustrate opponents. The American politician, however, has become a super-dissembler, one speaking not with a forked tongue but with a multiplicity of tongues. He has been forced into this role owing to the variegated composition of his constituency, composed of a great variety of ethnic and religious groups and economic and cultural classes.

In no European country except the Soviet Union is there such a great group variety, and in the Soviet Union these groups do not have untrammeled voting rights. All these groups in the United States listen to politicians with their ears attuned for special nuances. Words that to a fully acculturated American have a neutral tone may to many others have an ominous one. There is the case of a senatorial candidate who defeated his opponent by charging him to be "a full-fledged thespian" because the man had once been an actor. In a more local election, the winner charged that his opponent had gone to a school where he had been forced to matriculate, and before graduating had been obliged to show his thesis and then had been obliged to participate in a baccalaureate. That opponent was routed.

All cases of ignorance, it will be said. But everybody is ignorant in some respect, usually a major respect, and can be imposed upon.

Words have different nuances for different people and for the less educated, the vast majority, unfamiliar words often sound threatening. Again, acceptable words, indeed laudable words, take on menacing meanings through contextual applications. Thus the laudable word "liberal" has come to denote, for many, preferential promotion for unqualified or less qualified people because they have been culturally deprived either by circumstance or past legal restrictions.

Such objectors to the word "liberal" object to the hiring or promotion of unqualified people, whatever the reasons for lack of qualification. Many who thus object to the word are reciprocally called racists, which they may be or not. In any event, the word, in context, has altered its meaning.

Owing to the hidden dangers that lie in words, especially in the presence of many unacculturated people or those immersed in different cultures, American politicians must be extremely cautious in the way they use language, more cautious than those in countries with homogeneous bodies of citizens brought up in a common culture with a common language. The need for greater caution has led to a more stilted and formalistic use of language.

Hearing a virtuoso in crowd management like a Franklin Roosevelt or a John Kennedy, it is not easy to take in all of his correct references and implications but from the way the crowd reacts one can tell the speaker "has it all together," is making all "the right moves." One can see, too, why those who contested these virtuosos lost, and one may wonder why they didn't lose by a greater margin. In a certain way, then, a political campaign is like a piece of poetry, with a certain amount of obscurity or mystery surrounding why it works. A piece of poetry that is considered unsuccessful may seem to have all the ingredients of a successful poem but it may simply not work, may not lift the reader. Yet it may be technically perfect—perfect but dead.

Somebody might have beaten Franklin D. Roosevelt in one of his four successful presidential campaigns but that person simply did not show himself. Chance, too, plays a role in the election of certain people.

At any rate, it is the polyglot character of the American electorate that makes the utterances of American politicians as slippery as they are. A promise not to raise taxes turns out not to be a promise to avoid increasing tax collections by removing deductions prior to taxes, thereby increasing tax liabilities. No politician has yet promised not to change the tax structure in any way so as to increase the tax yield and one may gamble safely that none will do so.

A large segment of the electorate at all times neither knows nor cares about what is being discussed by candidates, in the end simply depending upon hunch for the decision in the voting booth. I myself have voted in every election since 1924—national, state and local—and although I always considered myself better informed about the candidates and issues than about 95 percent of the electorate (because I was always an assiduous reader), I rarely knew much about the candidates or how they would perform. This was just as true of congressional or local candidates as of national candidates.

The first presidential vote I ever cast was for Senator Robert M. La Follette of Wisconsin in 1924. I knew he had no chance of winning as he was at the time on a third-party ticket; but he had had a long and distinguished track record in office and I consider this the best vote I ever cast. John W. Davis, the Democratic candidate, had been a one-term congressman and had also served a term in the West Virginia House of Delegates, apart from which he had held appointive offices in the Wilson Administration and was mainly a corporation lawyer. The Republican candidate was Calvin Coolidge, an insignificant figure.

In 1928, I voted for Al Smith, Democrat, who had an extensive and favorable track record. The Republican candidate was Herbert Hoover, who had never before run for elective office. Hoover was a bureaucrat, and a good one, but was mainly carried into office on the basis of a synthetic life history as the appointed U.S. Food Administrator for postwar Europe and as a "great" engineer. Hoover was not connected with any notable engineering projects but had served for many years in foreign lands as a mining engineer although he held no engineering degree. However, reports still have it that he took an engineering degree. Not that it makes any difference.

I voted for Norman Thomas in 1932 although I was never a Socialist. But Roosevelt and the Democrats at the time were not addressing the topic of the Depression, no doubt feeling sure of beating the luckless Hoover. The Democrats at the time argued that the government was too large and spendthrift. No sign was in sight of the New Deal except possibly to deep insiders.

I voted for Roosevelt in 1936 and 1940, but for Thomas E. Dewey in 1944 and 1948, even though I believed he was a cocksure twerp. My reason for voting for him was that by now virtually all public offices, national, state and local, were held by Democrats and the country seemed in prospect of becoming a one-party country. To me this did not seem a healthy prospect as the system requires that the artful dodgers in officer ought to be watched at least by rivals outside. And outside rivals must have a chance to win.

From then on for four election and three Presidents—Eisenhower, Kennedy and Johnson—I voted for winners. Although I feel melancholy about voting for Kennedy and Johnson in view of their performances, I also felt I had little alternative in Richard Nixon and Barry Goldwater. I got Nixon's number as a thorough-going hypocrite at the time of his "Checkers" speech in 1952 and couldn't abide him thereafter. So I voted against him both times he won, and then voted against Gerald Ford in 1976, a Nixon clone. I voted for Ronald Reagan twice, not because I saw him as the nation's savior but because of the hypocritical charges brought against him by office-hungry Democratic Party people.

In my opinion none of the holders of the presidency after Eisenhower was really qualified to fill the office. Eisenhower's biggest mistake was keeping Nixon on the ticket in 1952, thereby inflicting him on the nation later. Kennedy inflicted Johnson. The sins of Presidents live and mature long after they leave the scene.

Looking backward, I can't see that any of my votes for President, or for any office-seeker, ever made a difference. As far as choice is concerned I would have made as good a choice most of the time by tossing a coin. Although I always knew far more about the candidates I voted for than did most of the public, my knowledge came from what was in print for the most part. In essence I knew about as much about the highly secretive members of the Soviet Politburo. Those fellows, like American candidates, also have synthetic life histories that detail prodigious accomplishments.

How Americans learn about their officialdom is by watching

their performance in office within the constitutional framework. In the matter of *post mortems*, Americans come out far ahead of the Russians. But by then it is always politically too late. It was so evident by 1968 that Lyndon B. Johnson was a disaster that he didn't even try for a second term, enamored though he was of holding the *imperium*.

Another advantage Americans have is that no branch of the government is in complete charge and even the Federal government must contend with at least three lower levels of government. But when a President like Johnson has a subservient Congress of his own party in his pocket, the country is positioned for disaster.

All of my voting experience has been in New York and Chicago, in New York City through 1952. There I had direct experience with city politics, which is notoriously corrupt. Except for the Fiorello La Guardia and John Lindsay, mayoral administrations in New York City have been corrupt at all levels since the end of World War I (leaving out of consideration previous years). Chicago has never enjoyed the saving grace of a La Guardia or Lindsay Administration.

Every close student of city government seems agreed that the situation in American cities has changed little, politically, since the publication of Lincoln Steffens' *The Shame of the Cities* (1904). Every serious investigation—and investigations are few and far between—results in another batch of officials going to jail or committing suicide when "caught with the goods."

The main reason is that the cities are heavily populated with what can only be described as displaced persons and economic refugees, from rural regions or from abroad. These people are in unfamiliar environments, dealing with unfamiliar problems and confronted by strange officials operating in a mysterious system. With a large portion of the constituency consisting of such elements the whole is easily manipulated by sharpers. Look where you will and you will find no sign of George Washington, Thomas Jefferson or Abraham Lincoln. The nearest to any of these will be the local party precinct captains, with very often only one party in the field.

Commenting on the idiotic content of American election campaigns, Willie Brown, the long-time Speaker of the California State Assembly, known for his frank comments, has said, "To win in this country these days you've got to campaign down to a 13-year-old's level of mental development."[1] Such a conclusion was hardly original with Speaker Brown but it shows what a candid operator thinks.

Brown did not mean that all of the electorate was of this level but just a large, significant portion of it, that large portion which educators find to be functionally illiterate. But it is precisely this part of the electorate that is sufficient to swing any election one way or the other, not that it makes much difference very often which candidate wins.

In 1968, it was Richard Nixon or Hubert Humphrey; in 1972, it was Nixon or George McGovern; in 1976, it was Jimmy Carter or Gerald Ford. And so on. Who would contend that the subsequent events would have been better if the loser had won? A little different perhaps, but not very different.

To suggestions that only fully qualified, educated voters should be allowed to vote, there is the instant mindless response of "elitism," followed by blustery objections. As to elitism I'll comment further along.

The late H. L. Mencken, with many agreeing with him, said the typical American voter was a "boob." To this description, defenders of the electoral system replied indignantly that Mencken was merely rude and unwarrantably pejorative. What Mencken meant by the boobishness of the "booboisie," to use one of his words, was their gullibility, their evident blind trust in preposterous third-raters making preposterous promises like Wilson's "war to end war." It was the enthusiasm of the crowd for obvious mountebanks that made Mencken term the members of the crowd boobs. Mencken knew that one set or the other of aspirants to office was going to win but he saw no need to suppose any of them were a reincarnation of Francis of Assisi, Florence Nightingale or Thomas Jefferson.

Mencken knew, too, that many Americans, wrought up by campaign oratory, actually wept when their candidate lost an election, usually a ludicrous spectacle of tears for a wholly fictitious character.

But the boobs are the true "swing" element in any election,

---

[1] *The New York Times*, October 31, 1988, B5:1-4.

cancelling the votes of any professors or similar "double domes" who may have voted the other ticket.

The United States Census Bureau ascertained who voted in the years 1984 and 1980, and found that of all persons registered, 42.9 percent with none to eight years of education voted, 44.4 percent of those with one to three years of high school voted, 58.7 percent of those with a high school diploma voted, 67.5 percent of those with one to three years of college voted, and 79.1 percent of those with four or more years of college voted. It was also found that those with larger incomes voted more often than others—under $5,000 only 37.5 percent of registrants; $10,000 to $15,000 as many as 53.5 percent; 61.1 percent of registrants for $20,000-$30,000 incomes, and 74.2 percent for incomes $35,000 upward.

The amount of formal education and family income, then, are powerful stimuli to voting, but the preponderance of numbers lies with the more deficient groups without whom nobody could win either a national election or a big-city election. The big-city political machines are notoriously corrupt and can elect just about anybody they have set their minds to elect, regardless of race, religion, sex or previous condition of desuetude. And regardless of total ignorance. Which of the big cities is the most corrupt?—a question that arises from time to time. A fairly safe rule of thumb, it seems to me, is to compute according to size, with New York the largest and Chicago next. Here the rule becomes: the larger the more corrupt. One reason for this is that the larger and more densely populated a city the more interstitial hiding places afforded officialdom. In such a labyrinth it is difficult to ascertain what anyone is really doing, where the revenues are being secretly tapped.

The only way I can think of to control big-city corruption under the present system is to have Federal grand juries, under fanatical prosecutors, sitting continuously and hearing charges and taking evidence against all local administrations. As these latter, however, are necessary to the success of national elections, such a procedure is not likely to be followed very long even though under the rivalrous two-party system. Under the Republican Reagan Administration, heavy Federal prosecutorial blows were struck against the Democrats in both New York City and Chicago.

It is a favorite tactic with much of the media to bring to light corruption abroad, especially in places like Mexico and Turkey. While all information about the world is useful, in some way it seems to me it would be better if more attention were paid to corruption at home, in the United States. There is enough political hanky-panky there, history shows, to keep any zealous anti-corruptionist busy for decades—if not centuries.

XVI

IT IS NOT my task to show ways of dealing with the problems touched upon. Nor do I seek or suggest any improvements or reforms. What I've attempted here is to clarify the idea that the United States—or any other western nation—is a democratic government because it is popularly elected. While an election may in itself be democratic, I contend that democracy stops at the point that each elected person takes the constitutional oath. From then on, the government is, in accordance with the Framers' intent, republican, independent in all its parts until the next election at least and very probably beyond.

It has been said that public opinion influences government and makes it democratic. While it is true that deep-rooted public opinion has an influence on government, the various members of the government usually share that public opinion, concealing any evidences of contrary views. But public opinion is complex and is subject to directed manipulation and influence. Such manipulation and influence may come from many quarters out in society but it also comes from government. It is a mistake to suppose that public opinion is self-formed and originating with a detached public. At least since the Creel Committee in the Wilson Administration, leading elements in almost every administration have delegated to special professional groups

140

within, however disguised they may have been, the task of shaping and manipulating public opinion. And this has been done apart from routine actions of government such as legislation or high court decisions that may have an impact on public opinion.

Almost everything that a government does has some impact on public opinion, calling forth a mild to strong reaction of approval or disapproval. Beyond this, formal attention to public opinion may shape it or turn it. Such attention, for example, may turn previously accepted groups into social pariahs, making them targets of animosity to their neighbors, as with German-Americans in 1917-18 and Japanese-Americans in 1941-42. Any group can thus be socially ostracized in pursuit of government policy and in flat contradiction to the spirit of the Constitution.

Very often the government completely orchestrates an entirely novel strain in public opinion, creating it out of a whole cloth. There may be dissidents but in almost all matters these are usually so few that like infinitesimals in calculus they can be ignored.

And in such circumstances—which always exist to some extent—the democracy outside the government becomes the puppet of the government more or less. And what is not achieved by propaganda can be achieved by coercion and direct force.

The 14th Amendment to the Constitution declares that all persons in the United States are entitled to "the equal protection of the laws." On the basis of this proviso, it is often argued that the aim of American society is egalitarianism, equality across the board. So to believe, however, is to overlook the fact that equality is far from the ideal of the citizenry in general.

American society, to the contrary, is probably the most elitist of any ever before seen in history. It is a society in which the champion, the winner, the star is publicly feted almost every day and the loser or routine performer is quickly pushed from sight and forgotten. One sees this in the constant adulation heaped on sports champions and celebrities, film stars, prize winners, Nobel laureates and the like. Crowds gather, mouths agape, at the rumor that one of these "stars" is around. "Look alikes" are frequently annoyed at being taken for "the real thing."

Such renown quickly translates into money at the box-office with the result that Americans are constantly entertained,

informed and diverted by a large coterie of box-office millionaires. At the same time spokesmen for the multitude inter-
mittently, on behalf of the multitude, decry the concentration
and maldistribution of wealth. What is overlooked here is that
everything is "unfairly" maldistributed—intelligence, beauty,
strength, agility, talent, health, and whatever else that is thought
most desirable.

Society, in practicing elitism while extolling equality, is
merely showing one of its numerous contradictions. It is these
native contradictions that leave the public open to manipulation
by people with special aims of their own. And being susceptible
to such manipulation, it is fundamentally powerless in any of the
areas that call for democratic power.

The situation, as between the manipulators and the manipulated, is similar to the one in wrestling where the very strength
of an opponent is used to subdue him. The democratic public is
always brought to the ground by its manipulators.

To all of which the true-blue, down-to-earth democrat will
object. Object he may, but he cannot, with the record before
him, refute it. Such a democrat often points to the "progress"
made by various groups in society, attributing such progress,
falsely, to democracy. An instance of such progress is the
improvement in the status of African-Americans, who were at
one time enslaved.

What is especially notable about the improvement in the
condition of this group, which is a fact, is in no way attributable
to democracy and was fought against all the way by the white
democratic rank and file—the democrats with the small "d" as
well as the Democrats with the Big D.

The gains in the status of African-Americans in the United
States came entirely from the republican government in one of
its many phases of ignoring the desires of the multitude. What
induced the republic, despite the views of most of its citizens, to
assist the blacks was less a desire to assist them than to assist
itself. It was "reasons of state" which at various times dictated the
policies of the government in this respect.

Such "reasons of state" have shown themselves at the following
crucial stages in this history:

1. The first of these "reasons of state" affecting African-
Americans was the Emancipation Proclamation, issued in Sep-

tember 1862, to take effect January 1, 1863. Its aim was to free "all slaves in areas still in rebellion." The Civil War had been raging since April 1861, and Lincoln's aim was to strike a blow at the South's capacity to wage war by freeing its slaves. The immediate result was a desertion of slaves to the Union forces, where they served in combat and labor battalions. The freeing of the slaves was the most severe single wartime blow levelled against the South by the northern Unionists.

2. The next stage in the freeing of America's blacks came with the passage of the 13th, 14th and 15th Amendments to the Constitution. The 13th Amendment, proposed in Congress and ratified by the states on December 18, 1865, abolished slavery or involuntary servitude except as a punishment for crime in all jurisdictions of the United States. The 14th Amendment, among other things, made all persons born or naturalized in the United States into citizens, which made blacks citizens. The 15th Amendment, ratified in 1870, declared that all male citizens had the right to vote, which could not be denied "on account of race, color, or previous condition of servitude."

Neither the Emancipation Proclamation nor the Amendments were ever submitted to a popular vote. Had they been they would not have been approved in the South and it is doubtful they would have been approved in the North. The purpose of none of these measures was to do any favors for the slave population. As indicated, the Proclamation was a hostile war measure against rebels in arms; the Constitutional Amendments were passed in order to break the power of the Democratic Party in the South. The granting of voting rights to African-Americans in the 15th Amendment had this purpose especially.

Even today, in a popular plebiscite, it may be doubted that all these measures would be approved. But if they were, there would surely be a large opposition. In any event, the electorate never had a chance to pass on any of them, which were all the product of President and Congress. The freeing of the slaves, then, and admitting them to citizenship, must be attributed to circumstances that led the government to free them for its own sake and for the sake of the Republican Party.

But the Republic giveth and the Republic taketh away, and African-Americans saw their gains diminished as a consequence of the presidential election of 1876. In that contest, Samuel J.

Tilden, of New York, Democrat, defeated Rutherford B. Hayes, of Ohio, Republican, by 4,287,670 votes to 4,035,924. This gave Tilden 184 Electoral College votes, one short of the required majority; Hayes had 165 electoral votes. But in doubt were the eight electoral votes of Louisiana, seven of South Carolina and four of Florida, and also one from Oregon.

Republicans refused to concede the election. At the time, the southern states were still under Unionist military occupation, all acts of southern state governments subject to military rescript. This meant that state control really lay with the Republicans in Washington. On any state vote recount, the report of boards to certify the election returns were all subject to military review.

According to the authoritative historian of the episode, C. Vann Woodward, not only were the state election boards dishonest but both political parties employed "irregularities, fraud, intimidation, and violence" to gain their way—and this remark may be extended to much of the history of elections in the United States, particularly in the larger cities. It should always be remembered that rival politicians are always contending for the *imperium* and all the plums that go with it.

The conclusion of historians is that in a fair election South Carolina and Louisiana would have been counted for Hayes but Tilden would have taken Florida and with it the presidency. But on December 6, 1876, electors for Hayes and Tilden met separately in the disputed states and cast their votes.

The disputed returns in Congress, to which the election was now referred, produced a deadlock between the Republican Senate and the Democratic House. But among the Democratic congressmen there were three overlapping groups willing to accept Hayes if their conditions were met. These conditions were the withdrawal of occupying troops from the South, restoration of prewar contacts between northern and southern businessmen and subsidies for the South similar to those given to northern railroads.

In the upshot, the dispute was referred to a congressional commission, which awarded all the disputed votes to Hayes. At this, Tilden supporters in Congress threatened a filibuster. Here the Hayes supporters opened negotiations with the southern Tilden supporters and reached informal agreements that if the filibuster was called off, Union troops would be withdrawn from the South and other southern demands would be given sympathetic consideration. As part of this deal, giving Hayes the presidency, the "Negro Question" was put into the hands of the southern states.

For some time the Jim Crow arrangement, or what South Africans now call *apartheid* or apartness, had been developing in the South and this arrangement now took wings. All public facilities throughout the South were now placed into African-American and white categories, with African-Americans invariably given subordinate or inferior facilities.

The Federal courts were brought into line with this arrangement. The Supreme Court began issuing a number of decisions in the 1880s that undermined the 14th and 15th Amendments with respect to African-Americans. In 1883, the Supreme Court declared the civil rights laws unconstitutional, and in 1896 came the famous *Plessy v. Ferguson* decision that decreed the constitutionality of "separate but equal" facilities as between whites and African-Americans. Unfortunately for judicial logic, there is no part of the Constitution that implies that people in society may be separated, except for those who have committed some crime and may be segregated in prison. The government, as it often does, was inventing constitutionality.

The African-Americans were now politically back approximately where they were under slavery except that they were technically free. In the South, *apartheid* was rigorously enforced and it was taken up informally in the North by trades unions and others. African-Americans throughout the North were informally barred from patronizing hotels, restaurants and other places of public accommodation, and in some places in the schools.

While the condition of African-Americans in the North was better than in the South, it was far from favorable as African-Americans were made to feel inferior at every turn and were freely challenged by police and others if they stepped out of their home ghettos.

3. All of this was suddenly cancelled in 1954 when the Supreme Court decided *Brown v. Board of Education*, holding that racial segregation in the public schools was unconstitutional as a violation of the 14th Amendment clause guaranteeing equal protection of the laws. This over-ruled *Plessy v. Ferguson*, flatly

and completely. If Plessy was wrong than everything based upon it was wrong.

In the eyes of some naive souls, the Supreme Court finally "understood" the Constitution on this point. What such souls fail to realize is that competent lawyers always and invariably fully understand the Constitution, do not make silly mistakes of misunderstanding plain language. The point is that politicians and their governments often do whatever they feel inclined at crucial moments to do, no matter what law or Constitution says.

What had caused the Court—and unanimously—to see the light in 1954? There was no demand for such a decision from the democratic mass. Nor was there, really, anything new about it because constitutional experts all had long agreed that *Plessy* was a deliberate misapplication of the Constitution.

But what had caused this reversal if not a sudden intellectual insight or a popular mass demand? There must have been some powerful coercive force at work and, as it happened, there was. The Cold War between the U.S. and the Soviet Union was in full force. The Soviet had exploded its first nuclear bomb and also the hydrogen bomb. The United States exploded its first hydrogen bomb in 1952, the Soviet Union in 1953.

The Soviet Union was on a full war footing, never really relaxed after World War II. And one thing it was doing, all over the world, was propagandizing about racial policy in the United States, how the American government believed that all people with dark skins were inferior and deserved to be humiliated and mistreated at every turn. The Soviet could support its case with an abundance of photographs from the United States showing Negroes being lynched and otherwise being mistreated, with no legal protection.

In a world where most people have dark skins, at least darker than white, such material was, from a political point of view, pure dynamite. The world situation seemed shaping up for war, and in this war the U.S. would have no friends among the darker races. Even short of war the U.S. was dependent in many ways on trade with people of darker hue—Japanese and East Indian and, as it finally turned out, Chinese. What American racial policy was doing was making enemies for itself throughout the world, embarrassing U.S. diplomats and business representatives in their tasks.

And the unyielding Soviet seemed ready to go as far as required to communize the world and rid it of hated capitalism.

This was the background against which the Supreme Court met to consider the case of *Brown v. Board of Education*. Now, the Supreme Court consists not only of lawyers, people versed in the labyrinths of the Constitution, but also of patriots of the Republic, one nation indivisible claiming liberty and justice for all. These people know more than what is set forth in the Constitution and the law books. They know what is going on in the world. And they know when a deadly weapon is being levelled at the United States.

At the time of the *Plessy* decision, the Supreme Court had in mind, obviously, more than the Constitution. It was aware of the demand by a large portion of American society for the segregation of the Negro. Again, in 1954, the members of the Court had before them more than the Constitution. They were aware of an enveloping world situation perilous to the United States. And, like patriots, they sought to do something about it.

What I am saying is that the Court did not act owing to some new-found knowledge of the Constitution or suddenly discovered fondness for African-Americans. The members of the Court were not, very definitely, "nigger lovers." The Court had many members who had ascended via the ladder of party politics. Earl Warren, the Chief Justice, had been governor of California and was the Republican vice-presidential nominee of 1948. Hugo L. Black, William O. Douglas, Harold H. Burton, Tom C. Clark and Robert H. Jackson were justices who all had held elective or appointive offices. They were all men who had a keen appreciation of what was going on in the world, particularly as it concerned the United States.

So, in looking for the motivations for the decision *Brown v. Board of Education*, while it is no doubt true that, as in all things, there were many factors at work, for the main factor one must look to the Kremlin. One possible source that played no role whatever was what is often magniloquently alluded to as "the great American democracy."

In point of fact there was great and continuing opposition to the decision of the Court out in society, and to implementation of the order by school busing of pupils to break the back of segregation. While the government, against popular opposition, was able to end segregation where it had been institutionalized, it was not able to end it among the people, the democratic mass. This was shown particularly by "white flight" that ensued when African-Americans, under the protection of the law, were allowed to move into "white" neighborhoods. Whites simply left the cities and moved into new suburbs, abandoning long-established churches, schools and other institutions. Crazy!

Had it been left to a plebiscite of the population, African-Americans would still be picking cotton in the South or would be engaged in similar menial tasks, barred from the educational system. This is a fact that can be deduced from majority white behavior toward African-Americans even today, shrinking from contact with them like the plague.

All of this is generally interpreted as showing a deep antipathy of whites toward African-Americans particularly and I wish now to challenge this notion by pointing to the antipathies of American whites among themselves along ethnic, religious and cultural lines. American whites all came from Europe, which was long the scene of struggle among a large variety of tribal groups. What is referred to as racism, peculiarly a white-black phenomenon, is really a part of tribalism, which prevails among whites as well as all others.

But the black-white animosity, stemming from the original subordinate position of African-Americans, has been to a considerable extent sharpened by the common opposition to the African-Americans which has served to solidify the whites as a unity. In other words, African-Americans have unconsciously performed the historical service of helping unify American whites, to make them conscious of being white rather than something else, such as Ruthenian or Croatian.

As one born and raised early in this century in Chicago, a city composed of just about all the immigrant groups, I had an opportunity to watch this white tribalism at first hand. Every white group, except the Anglo-Saxon and Scotch, was referred to in Chicago by every other white by some demeaning pejorative term, usually used matter-of-factly or even amiably, the way a southerner often used the term "nigger." But there was often animosity between immigrant groups, shown particularly in their sense of possessing their neighborhoods. The city was like a crazy-quilt of immigrant communities, some as much as a mile square or more.

With the incursion of the African-Americans in large numbers, particularly after the latest Supreme Court decisions striking at segregation, the city saw "white flight" at its most panic-stricken. Most of the great South Side and just about as much of the West Side, all once largely white ethnic, was surrendered to the African-Americans and the whites dispersed to the suburbs. It is now a case of the niggers living in place of the dagoes, wops, ginneys, sheenies, kikes, yids, bohunks, hunyaks, polacks, krauts, squareheads, spics and even chinks. Such was standard daily language of the day.

There were, too, the micks and the turks, as the Irish were commonly known.

And while conflict among the white ethnics was never as severe as between blacks and whites (who were often involved in bloody race riots), it could nevertheless eventuate in fighting, especially among male youths. The Irish seemed the most belligerent, living up to the legend of "the fighting Irish," but others could be stirred into similar behavior. And who started the trouble was always a question, involving charges and counter-charges.

The pejorative term WASP (for white Anglo-Saxon Protestant) was not yet current or it would no doubt have been applied to the more established elements that ran the city from the big banks and corporations and occupied its more affluent neighborhoods. But most of the city, as today, was far from affluent although most of the areas since surrendered to the African-Americans were in much better shape than they are today.

Now, Chicago was not exceptional. It was typical of the largest American cities and, on a more emphatic note, of the entire country. New York City was even more tribalistic and to this day exhibits its tribalism by way of formal parades—the St. Patrick's Day parade for the Irish Catholics, Columbus Day parade for the Italians, Steuben Day parade for the Germans, Pulaski Day parade for Poles. The Puerto Ricans have also taken to parading and a small Norwegian group in Brooklyn likes to parade. The Greeks, too, have their parade.

These tribal parades, incidentally, have the practical political purpose of exhibiting voting groups to politicians, making them more amenable from time to time to tribal leaders.

The various ethnic groups that came to this country from Europe had a long history of mutual animosities developed in the

European cockpit. It was not something that flowered for the first time in the United States where it was in fact gradually muted. But some of it remained. The politicians' vision of the happy melting pot in which many immigrant groups took refuge from harsh conditions abroad was a piece of fiction. And most newcomers met with sufficiently harsh conditions here in the politicians' golden land of plenty. Not even one-tenth of one percent of the immigrants, or the children of immigrants, ever became so much as a congressman or a city alderman. That road was always very crowded. And while some became millionaires, these were not numerous.

As to African-American tribalism, this never had a chance to show itself in America in the common disaster of slavery. But if we turn to Africa we find it rampant with one tribe slaughtering members of another by the thousands, and even today—men, women, children, infants. African-Americans, if they resettled in Africa, might find they were up against tribalism of a more savage nature than they find in the United States.

Who, in the United States, is not a tribalist? In my own observation, I have seen the hold of tribalism least among the well-schooled and well-read. Apart from these it is as pervasive as religion. One finds it in the idiotic expression, "I am proud to be a So-and-So."

In any event, the deliverance of the African-Americans from their political shackles up to the decision in *Brown v. Board of Education* all came from the government unilaterally, against strong white protest. The whites were too stupid to see that the government was really acting in their interest from a world-political point of view. But the government had not always been so favorable to the African-Americans. In the Wilson Admin-istration, for example, Josephus Daniels, Secretary of the Navy, reduced the status of African-Americans in the Navy, which had long been something of a safe harbor for them. Daniels ordered that African-Americans were henceforth to serve only as cooks, waiters and roustabouts—a present from the Democratic Party!

The decision in *Brown v. Board of Education*, holding African-Americans entitled to the same consideration as whites, had the effect of emboldening African-Americans to challenge southern *apartheid*. Early in 1960, African-Americans refused to leave a lunch counter in Greensboro, N.C., when denied service and the so-called civil rights movement was launched. The Kennedy Administration, and after it the Johnson Administration, showed sympathy for black demands, and in June 1964, an omnibus civil rights bill was passed that barred discrimination against African-Americans in voting, employment, public accommodations and elsewhere. A new Voting Rights Act was passed in 1965.

In 1967, black rioting broke out in Newark, Detroit and other cities, with many killed and much arson and looting as paratroopers and National Guards were called in. President Johnson meanwhîle had appointed Thurgood Marshall, a black, to the Supreme Court, where he took his place in October. Johnson, too, had proclaimed his "Great Society" program, in which African-Americans were also to participate.

All this sudden bustle on behalf of African-Americans by Democratic national leaders was to impede the future of the Democratic Party nationally. For from 1968 onward, the Democrats won the White House only once out of six elections through 1988. There was evident "white flight" from the Democratic Party, especially in the once Solid South. But there was such flight elsewhere, too, as shown by the emergence of "Reagan Democrats, " who were Democrats that voted Republican. These were angry, among other things, about having African-Americans jostle them for jobs.

I have been at some pains to trace the steps releasing African-Americans from bondage in order to show that such release came from government acting against the demands of the general populace, one more obvious proof that the government does not act according to the wishes of a majority of the populace. I have shown that the government often does this, sometimes unconstitutionally, sometimes lying to the populace as in overthrowing foreign governments on trumped-up charges of communism or in inventing incidents like that of Tonkin Gulf, but also quite constitutionally as in the handling of the African-Americans.

Whether legal or illegal, constitutional or unconstitutional, the government usually acts according to its own internal counsel. The option of the electorate, of course, is to vote against any officials that offend it or seem about to offend it. And it is here that democratic power can show itself, in the choice of officials. But this democratic power has no effect on Federal court decisions, which state the law. As bone-deep Republicans like to say, "We live under a government of laws, not men." That is, ultimately under court decisions.

At certain stages, the power of the electorate in rejecting a set of officials is supreme. This was shown, for example, in 1932, when the Hoover Administration and Republicans across the country were swept from office. The electoral complaint here was the sudden loss of jobs for 25 percent of the labor force. It became axiomatic in American politics thereafter that a high rate of unemployment will unseat incumbent officials forthwith, which has led to government programs of insurance for the jobless. Without a job or money coming from some other source, anyone is a hopeless cripple in American society.

There are other matters, too, in which the electorate can act punitively against incumbents, as it was about to act in 1968 against Lyndon B. Johnson until he declined to seek reelection.

XVII

ENOUGH HAS BEEN SET FORTH in this extended essay to exhibit the strength of my thesis that the claim that we live under a democratic government is so much humbug, a tantalizing fiction. I could go on for 1,000 pages to cite supporting data to show that the government usually acts on the basis of its own inspiration, without being instructed by the populace. I forebear doing this.

Nothing of what I have written would be astonishing to members of the original Constitutional Convention in Philadelphia, most of whom felt the populace was too confused and divided to be able to govern democratically. As they saw it, democracy was practical only on a very small scale, as in the New England towns, but would never be able to function on an extended scale.

What the Framers thought then, with a largely homogeneous population (except for the African-Americans), is applicable with multiplied force today when the country has become literally polyglot, with many people unable to speak simple English and militantly resistant even to making English the official language. There is, in fact, little that the population as a whole agrees upon within itself. What the American population needs to make it effective is the government. Without that it is an inchoate mob. There is no need for politicians to apply the Roman principle of "divide and rule." It is already divided into as many pieces as a jigsaw puzzle.

What the American people have as a principal asset, in addition to the land itself and its climate, is the Constitution, which stands there as a ready-made bed to fall into from time to time. It is not necessary to see the Constitution as the acme of perfection, as some profess to do, to be aware of its great utility. The difference between constitutionalism, with whatever defects, and the diverse projects of the masses is the difference between order and pure chaos.

The Constitution was devised as a practical instrument, without any professions of being a world-saving or soul-saving instrumentality. It was, first, to provide offices of "honor and profit"—especially the latter. Here was an appeal to acquisitiveness and egotism, two powerful human propensities. The result is that there is never a lack of claimants to office in the United States. In fact, there is a long line in wait for every office down to the lowest one in the states.

That the offices are directly profitable shows up in the fact that for most of the occupants, from congressman to President, the offices pay more than any of them ever earned in private life. As Emerson noted in the mid-19th century, office-seeking itself has become a trade. The politician and his followers are all instinctive jobholders.

So citizens may always be sure that the government is fully staffed. Honor and profit are the lures.

And once staffed, the government is so laid out that the personnel must in most respects follow broad lines of behavior or be ousted by means of mechanisms brought into play by the same self-interest that leads to the staffing of the government. The lines of behavior to be followed are laid out in the Constitution.

What we see now is seldom a perfect government. But we do see at the very least an operating government, and one that is not being frequently overthrown, as with many European parliamentary governments. Congressmen are in for two years, Senators for six and Presidents for four, with Federal judges installed for life (during "good behavior").

It is far from true that this government always turns in a

satisfactory performance. But when it does not it may be gradually dismantled and all of its personnel replaced within the space of six years. The entire House of Representatives can be voted out in two years, one third of the Senate in each two years up to six and the President every four years. The population, in short, has an ultimate say in who remains in government.

This ultimate say, however, does not mean that the population dictates policy to the government. I have shown abundantly that it does not. The government does whatever it thinks necessary, as when it deals Negroes either into or out of the system, and the electorate can take it or complain about it. But in the face of a court decision, the electorate has no recourse except usually futile protest. Some in the electorate, in fact, are life-long dissidents, objecting to everything the government does.

I don't mean to suggest that there is anything like an Iron Curtain between the government and the populace. There is an interplay between the two, with the government always coming out on top. When push comes to shove, the government prevails.

This has been shown in the case of white segregated residential areas. Once the government ruled these as taboo, we saw the rulings followed by "white flight." But the areas to which whites fled are just as open to African-Americans willing to follow there as were the original areas. There are now some leading suburbs where blacks live harmoniously with whites.

That, we may say, is a triumph of republican constitutionalism and counter to original white democratic inclination. As I noted earlier, Thomas Jefferson founded the Democratic Party as an instrument of opposition to the original Federalists. But this party soon degenerated into the instrument of the southern slavocracy, then into the tool of wildly destructive rebellion and finally as the producer of *apartheid*.

It is only in recent decades that the Democratic Party has attempted to change its orientation, thereby losing the support of many white tribalists. But as far as the promotion of democracy is concerned, the Democratic Party all along, in all its phases, has been a huge failure because, as the Framers recognized, what it originally attempted to realize—democratic rule—is impossible beyond a limited territory.

The ancient Greeks, credited with inventing democracy, were themselves practitioners of *apartheid* on a colossal scale. They definitely did not include all men in their democratic circle as they regarded all non-Greeks as barbarians, uncouth and loutish. Numbered among such barbarians were all the non-Greek inhabitants of the Italian peninsula as well as all other European peoples—all of whom were destined to out-do the Greeks in cultural achievements. The Greeks invented many things, such as philosophy and science, that later non-Greek Europeans—and others—perfected and carried to heights beyond the Greek imagination. So much for barbarians.

Now, nothing I have written calls for any change in behavior by anybody, any reform of any institution or any new taxation. It does, however, require a change in one's thinking and general political orientation. It requires one to see that the government is not, in fact, democratic in any sense of the word merely because it may be democratically elected (apart from its judges).

This may be seen by some as a trivial point but on the question of who is directing the government it is far from trivial but, in fact, crucial. Although the United States government is directed by popularly elected personnel, acting under constitutional precepts, concrete events and decisions show that the popular mood does not control the government, which acts according to its own collective determination, often against the prevailing opinion among the masses. And this is what the Framers intended.

To believe otherwise is to be deceived, as many are under the steady propaganda that the government is a democracy—the greatest democracy on earth and the greatest that will ever be seen or is imaginable. At any rate, greatest.

But for anyone who wants to think clearly with respect to politics and government, none of this is so. It is pure pipe dream. In saying this, I am much in the same position as the little boy in the story of the emperor's new clothes. The little boy discerned that the emperor was, in fact, naked.

What makes the idea of democracy so popular and well-received is that it is so flattering. It is far from flattering to realize that one is doing something because one is ordered to do it by the government, such as treating darker-skinned persons with ordinary civility. Yet Americans are obliged, under penalty of law, to behave in many ways that are popularly resented. More than three million who refuse to do so are under what is known as "correctional supervision"—that is, in jail, prison, on parole or probation.[1]

But large numbers not under such supervision are forced against their will to function in certain ways, under the threatening penalty of law that would be changed if it were up to the electorate. There is surely nothing democratic about that.

It will no doubt also be said by some that I am merely wrangling about the meanings of words, and that the meanings of words change historically. This last is true but the meaning of a word like "democracy" has not changed. What has happened, however, is that it is being misapplied. There is evidently a great yearning out in society for this word to be used, and this yearning is seen in Professor Sidney Hook's contention that what we have in the U.S. republic is "indirect democracy." Hook is smart enough to know we have nothing like direct democracy except in places like New England towns, but because two out of three divisions of the government are popularly elected, he wishes to have it that these elected people do the popular bidding. Sometimes they may do so, but often they do not, which is what the Framers explicitly intended. And although the Framers incorporated slavery into the Constitution, they also left the road open to its abolition. For they knew that government must adjust to changing circumstances.

I must say that I hardly expect media people, if any of them read these pages, to stop referring to "the American democratic government," although they could improve a bit by inserting the word "so-called" and changing nothing else. But so habitual has it become to term the government a democracy, rather than correctly as a republic, that one may well doubt any change of phrasing, at least in the near term.

Just how ridiculous the use of the term "democratic" can be we find by turning to the German Democratic Republic, as East Germany is now known. To paraphrase the historian Edward Gibbon in his reference to the Holy Roman Empire, the German Democratic Republic is neither German, nor democratic, nor a republic. What it is is a territory captured by the Soviet Union and managed by German Soviet puppets, backed by the Soviet

---

[1]*U.S. Statistical Abstract*, 1988, pp. 176-177.

Army. None of the many Soviet so-called republics is a true republic in view of the fact that each is under tyrannical rule, in the presence of which anything like a republic is impossible.

The United States is in fact a republic, as is France. Great Britain, which calls itself a constitutional monarchy, also measures up to all the requirements of a republic. Neither France nor Great Britain are democracies, as is widely claimed in the modern rage of people to imagine they are self-ruled.

And although the Constitution of the United States mentions many things, it nowhere mentions the word democracy.

XVIII

AND NOW IT MAY BE WELL to review briefly the extent to which the government acts either without any demand from the electorate or contrary to such demand.

In 1912, as we have noted, a split in the Republican Party, then a majority, permitted the election of Woodrow Wilson as President by a minority. In this first administration, Wilson produced what scholars concede was excellent reform—most of it unasked for by most of the electorate.

Wilson was elected for a second term in 1916 on the basis of wholesale falsification about the war in Europe and implied promises to stay out of the war, as well as denials that plans were being drawn up for conscription of young males or that there were unprecedented plans to send them into combat abraod. The entire Wilson second term went against majority sentiment in the country and widespread dissidence was met by widespread unconstitutional violence on the part of government agents.

In 1918 and in three national elections—1920, 1924 and 1928—the Democratic Party was routed. The basic issue in all three campaigns was to keep the Democrats out.

In 1932, there was an abrupt about-face in the voters' mood as President Herbert Hoover, Republican, was resoundingly rejected in a landslide victory for the Democrats. What had caused this change in mood was the unemployment of a quarter of the labor force, leaving millions without any money in a money economy. Although Hoover had taken steps to shore up government operations, he had stopped short of direct aid for the multitudes who were stricken as by an invisible plague.

But no part of the New Deal program the Democrats put into force under President Franklin D. Roosevelt had been before the electorate during the election. The New Deal that ensued was a complete and pleasant surprise to the multitude. That the electorate in general liked what was done is reflected in the fact that Roosevelt was re-elected for an unprecedented three times and the Democratic Party held control of the White House for five terms.

Yet nothing of what was done was antecedently passed upon by the electorate, which was as ignorant of what was to come as was the electorate of 1916. To speak about it all as though there was a democratic control of coming events is to perpetrate a fiction.

Dwight D. Eisenhower was nominated for President by the Republican Party in 1952 mainly because he was a war hero opposed by a nationally unknown Democrat, Adlai E. Stevenson. Neither candidate had any particular program to lay before the electorate although Eisenhower did promise to end the Korean War, a promise he fulfilled.

From 1960 onward, through the elections of 1964, 1968, and 1972, deception and falsification was the order of the day for the winning candidates, all of whom gave the country unpleasant events that the electorate had never ordered. Kennedy in 1960, promising to "get the country moving again," whatever that meant, and pointing to a dangerous "missile gap" between Soviet and American forces, a falsehood, defeated Republican Richard Nixon, a case where the electorate had little choice. In 1964, Lyndon Johnson, Democrat, attacked Barry Goldwater, Republican, as a warmonger, implying that he himself was a man of peace. There was no hint in any of his expressions that he intended to escalate the Vietnam War.

American forces had been put into Vietnam by President Kennedy, who had no mandate from the electorate to do anything of the sort. Neither Kennedy nor Johnson, nor Nixon after them, had any electoral mandate to do anything they did that was special to their administration. Nixon had no mandate to make friends with China, a complete surprise.

Nixon the Republican was elected in 1968, saying he had a "plan" that would get the country out of Vietnam "with honor." There was no plan. The pledge was so much empty talk and the war rolled on destructively until 1973, with American forces finally withdrawn in an ignominious retreat visible to everybody on television.

All these Presidents—Kennedy, Johnson, Nixon and Gerald Ford at the end of the procession—were simply childish, with far less grasp of world affairs than any of the least experienced newsmen around them. They not only had little notion of the effects of their various actions but were patently bewildered pretenders. Their proper arena was big-city municipal politics, there to make deals with aldermen and local contractors.

The record is not yet complete on Ronald Reagan, who took over the presidency in 1960 and kept his popularity until the very end, which is unusual for a two-term President. But it appears that Reagan upon leaving office could, as I have suggested already, well echo Louis XIV and say, "Apres moi, le deluge." For enormously explosive problems have been left behind.

There was widespread complaint about the election of 1988 that the candidates did not address the issues. This is true. But presidential candidates since Wilson rarely do address the issues although they may create fictional issues like Kennedy's "missile gap."

And what goes on with respect to the presidential office more or less also goes on with respect to lesser offices, Federal, state and local. The electorate knows little about the men running for office and less about what they will do once they have taken the solemn oath of office. In view of their behavior it may be surmised that many take this oath with fingers crossed.

About most of what is contemplated in government, at all levels, the electorate usually has little inkling. One development after another comes as a surprise, often disbelieved on being first reported. That the public is being constantly manipulated is shown by the way unfavorable news, at all levels, is as much as possible delayed until just after an election. Then the public cannot strike back at their manipulators; later the public will have forgotten, preoccupied with some newly visible problem.

To suggest that any of this conforms to democratic precepts is to show little comprehension of what is taking place. To believe any of it is in any sense democratic is to reveal total confusion of mind.

In closing, let us take a final look at elections. In most of these, enough flagrant errors are made in logic, semantics and factuality by the chief partisans to merit expulsion from any standard college or university. Yet most of the people running election campaigns are college graduates. What they do is tailor their messages to conform to the understanding of the voting mass. The mixture turns out, on examination, to be the purest sophistry and the election result is invariably hailed as one more triumph for democracy.